# BASICS
## GRAPHIC DESIGN
### 02

Neil Leonard
Gavin Ambrose

# Design
# Research

Investigation for successful creative solutions

**Ethical:** aware-
ness/
reflect-
ion/
debate

academia

**An AVA Book**

Published by AVA Publishing SA
Rue des Fontenailles 16
Case Postale
1000 Lausanne 6
Switzerland
Tel: +41 786 005 109
Email: enquiries@avab

Distributed by Thames
(ex-North America)
181a High Holborn
London WC1V 7QX
United Kingdom
Tel: +44 20 7845 5000
Fax: +44 20 7845 5055
Email: sales@thameshudson.co.uk
www.thamesandhudson.com

Distributed in the USA & Canada by:
Ingram Publisher Services Inc.
1 Ingram Blvd.
La Vergne TN 37086
USA
Tel: +1 866 400 5351
Fax: +1 800 838 1149
Email: customer.service@
ingrampublisherservices.com

English Language Support Office
AVA Publishing (UK) Ltd.
Tel: +44 1903 204 455
Email: enquiries@avabooks.com

ISBN 978-2-940411-74-0

Library of Congress Cataloging-in-
Publication Data
Leonard, Neil; Ambrose, Gavin.
Basics Graphic Design 02: Design
Research. / Neil Leonard; Gavin
Ambrose. p. cm.
Includes bibliographical references
and index.
ISBN: 9782940411740 (pbk. :alk.
paper)
eISBN: 9782940447381
1. Graphic arts. 2. Commercial arts.
NC997 .L465 2012

10 9 8 7 6 5 4 3 2 1

Design by Gavin Ambrose
Cover image by Fuse Collective

Production by AVA Book Production
Pte. Ltd., Singapore
Tel: +65 6334 8173
Fax: +65 6259 9830
Email: production@avabooks.com.sg

0.1
**Your opinion is irrelevant
because I hate you**
*Hannah Richards* (a student at
the University of Brighton, UK)

Developing a sense of style and a
confidence in your work takes time.
This engaging epigram, 'This is the
way to the thing you insisted you
needed to see even though I have
described it to you in great detail',
is part of a larger body of work by
Hannah, shown on page 138.

THIS IS THE WAY
TO THE THING
YOU INSISTED YOU
NEEDED TO SEE
EVEN THOUGH I
HAVE DESCRIBED IT
TO YOU IN GREAT
DETAIL

# Contents

**6 Introduction**

**8 Chapter 1 / The basics of research**

10 Why research?
12 Getting started
18 Primary, secondary and tertiary
26 Key terminology
32 Studio interview: Emily Hale
34 Activity: Approaching research

**36 Chapter 2 / Understanding context**

38 Audience and social contexts
50 Design contexts
60 Theoretical underpinning
64 Studio interview: Andrew Hussey
66 Activity: Convention

**68 Chapter 3 / Planning your work**

70 The brief
76 Audience
78 Sources and credibility
82 Recording and documenting
90 Studio interview: Brian Rea
92 Activity: Audience

**94 Chapter 4 / Conducting research**

**96** Audience research
**106** Market research
**112** Field-based research
**120** Process-based research
**122** Studio interview: Jane Trustram
**124** Activity: Product and customer


**126 Chapter 5 / Using your findings**

**128** Understanding your findings
**134** Responding to your findings
**152** Studio interview: Underware
**154** Activity: Classification


**156 Chapter 6 / Presenting your findings**

**158** Presenting research
**176** Completing the job
**182** Studio interview: Tanner Christensen
**184** Activity: Presenting statistics


**186 Conclusion**
**187 Contacts**
**188 Bibliography**
**190 Index**
**192 Acknowledgements**
**193 Working with ethics**

**A graphic design project can be viewed as a series of choices – the more informed these choices are, the stronger the outcome will be. Research is the tool that, above all others, can help you gain the in-depth knowledge needed to inform your choices and make the most appropriate and educated decisions.**

Research is an ongoing process, beginning with initial fact-finding as you respond to a brief, and progressing through audience research, to the development and synthesis of ideas, and the final testing of materials, processes and resolutions.

The processes you undertake may be structured or intuitive, but all research should be approached with an open mind. You may start with a very clear methodology that allows you to move from one step to another in a structured way, or you may prefer to engage in a series of experiments and allow the outcome of these to dictate your next step. In either case, you should be open to what your research tells you.

This book will act as a guide, introducing you to relevant concepts and terminology, and helping you make the most of your investigative work. The chapters help you discover appropriate research methods, identify and question your target market and make appropriate and targeted design choices. The book will help you make the best of your creative ideas, formulate plans and structure your work in a way that will benefit your final ideas and open fresh avenues of creativity.

0.2
**The Blight of Natural Catastrophe**
*Tom Clohosy Cole*

Shown is a gouache illustration for a university project exploring a fictional insurance company. Tom explains, 'I approach research in a variety of ways. Once I have an idea, I like to discuss it with as many people as I can. I find the ideas and recommendations of other people an invaluable resource in starting to construct an idea or body of work as they often lead down paths I would not have strayed down.'

Research is to see what everybody else has seen, and to think what nobody else has thought.

Albert Szent-Gyorgyi

0.2

## Chapter 1 – The basics of research

**Understanding the need for research, the techniques available and the possibilities that each of these offer is key to becoming a well-informed designer.**

In this chapter we consider the initial stages of research, looking at the starting points that will guide later activities. Basic terminology that describes broad types of research is introduced, with examples of how these can be used within your projects. We then explore more complex terminology and relate this to relevant supporting theories.

**Research drives a design project – it gives you direction and focus as well as determining the quality of your outcomes. Graphic design is a form of problem solving and the tools needed to arrive at the solution will be found by conducting research. Simply put, good research equals good design.**

By looking at the different types of research detailed in this book, you will be able to determine ways each can be usefully employed at various points during your projects. These stages range from initial observational work, to understanding your audience, as well as the testing of materials, processes and ideas. The key with all research is to be active throughout the process and allow the results to take you beyond what you already know. There are several paths you may choose to follow and your research can be based around practice, experimentation or theory, and all are equally valid.

The best research happens when you put yourself in the place of your audience by interacting with this group and familiarizing yourself with the context of your project as thoroughly as possible. This level of research requires you to be active and open to lines of enquiry suggested by the people you engage with.

Research will also help you to determine the best way for a piece of design to be produced; by looking closely at the use and cost of materials you can often offer design solutions that are well produced and cost effective.

**1.1**
**The Energy Within Me**
*StudioKxx*

StudioKxx's approach to typography reflects trends in film and culture. It also, as a pioneer, sets the trend for others to follow. The example opposite was created in response to an invitation from Coca Cola to artists worldwide to create an original interpretation of the phrase 'Energizing refreshment'.

The resulting typographic form, rendered by designer Piotr Buczkowski, is an amalgamation of several layers of typographic treatments. Research for the project involved finding examples of expressive typographic treatments, including the work of Psyop and Grandpeople, and also exploring and experimenting with typographical expression.

# Research is the act of going up alleys to see if they are blind.

Plutarch

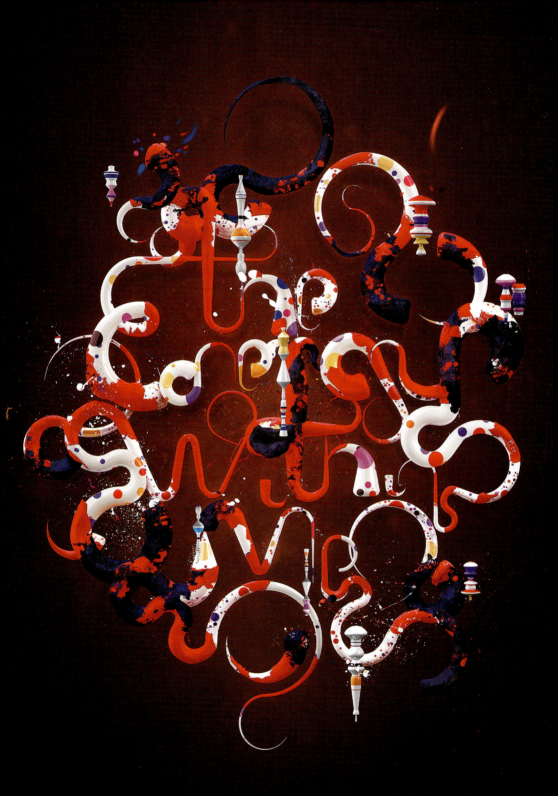

**The most basic qualities any designer needs are an inquisitive nature and the desire to make things better. It is the designer's job to raise public awareness of ideas, products and services, and to constantly innovate by finding new solutions to old problems whilst reacting to contemporary expectations. The issues associated with each project will vary greatly and research is vital to ensuring that the problem is fully understood and the best possible solution is offered.**

When you start researching a project, you will need to think about where relevant information that will be used to inform your design decisions can be accessed. There are a huge number of potential sources, and with the Internet it is now straightforward to access a large amount of information on just about any subject.

If you are gathering factual and statistical information, the most reliable source is still the library. Most libraries have current periodicals, databases and access to large archives of academic texts, newspapers and books. Many newspaper archives will have papers over a hundred years old in print form or saved on microfilm. Much of this historical information has not yet been digitized, so this is often the only way to access it.

Local authorities will hold valuable information regarding the local population, such as migration, income and population statistics. Nationwide information of this sort can be sourced through government websites, and will provide you with a broad perspective, and a comparison for any targeted group you are researching.

1.2
**Joupii packaging design**
*Webb & Webb*

Joupii is a premium wooden toy that was first produced in the 1960s. Originally manufactured by Naef Spiele in Switzerland by hand, Joupii is now made by Il Leccio wooden toys in Italy. James Webb explains the process behind this design: 'Joupii's packaging needed to be as beautiful, natural in materials and as simple as the toy. Printing in black only on premium Italian board, the pattern of Joupiis show the posable nature of the toy. Using kiss-cut stickers as the only colour photographic element meant we could distinguish the toy's body colour – red, yellow, green or blue – by simply changing the label design on the box. The Joupii logotype was drawn to emphasize the toy's most distinguishing feature – his round head and eyes.'

1.2

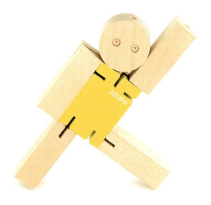

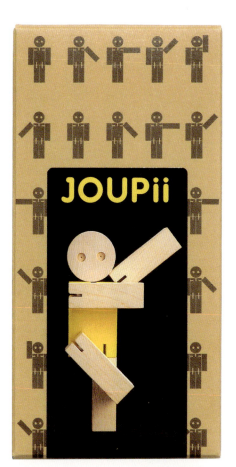

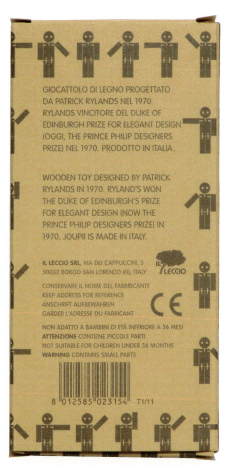

## Preparatory research

The ways that you can approach research vary greatly, depending on the type and scale of your project. Large jobs may require intensive research, whereas smaller day-to-day jobs can sometimes be approached with existing knowledge. Usually, a designer will consider this when they are pitching for a job, and build research time into the hours expected to complete the job.

Once a job has been offered, it is good practice to research the client before the brief has been sent. This will help you identify whether this is a job you will be able to pursue, and also give context to the expected outcomes. Once you have done this, look at their customer base. Again, this will help you assess the brief, and may suggest a range of criteria, from the likely prestige and scale of the work, to use of materials and choice of processes.

**Pitching for a job**
It is rare for a designer to be offered a job outright. Normally, a client will ask several designers to present their ideas for how they might solve the brief – this is the pitch. A successful pitch requires a lot of time and energy as a lot hinges on it.

## Overview and observation

One of the first things you can do to gain an overview when starting a new project is to look at work that has already been created in the area you are researching. When looking to the work of others for inspiration, start broadly and then identify what is of most relevance. It can be tempting to start by looking at work you are already familiar with, but it is best to look at where your final designs will be seen and use this context as the foundation of your investigation. When you find something useful, investigate who created it and look for their other work and their influences. An overview of existing design in the area you will be working in is important, as it will indicate possible parameters or elements that you could improve upon.

Observation is another preparatory research method, used to gain an initial understanding of a subject. It may be an active process or one of contemplation, but should be carefully considered. Your initial observations will often form the basis of your approach and may figure in decisions about your methodology later on.

**1.3**

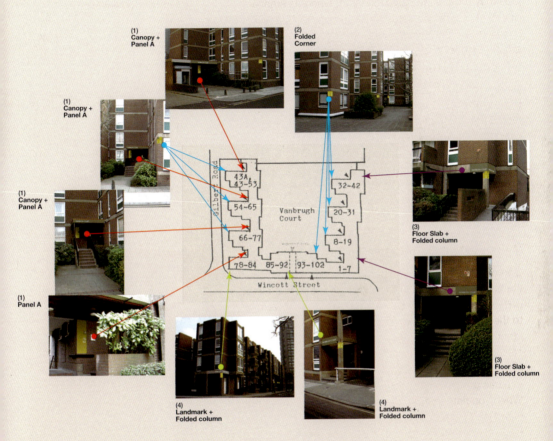

(1)
Canopy +
Panel A

(2)
Folded
Corner

(1)
Canopy +
Panel A

(1)
Canopy +
Panel A

(1)
Panel A

(3)
Floor Slab +
Folded column

(3)
Floor Slab +
Folded column

(4)
Landmark +
Folded column

(4)
Landmark +
Folded column

## 1.3
## Vanbrugh Court
### *Studio AS*

Vanbrugh Court is a residential development that was built in three phases during the 1970s in Kennington, London. Following consultations on the needs of the tenants, access and security were redefined. As a result, new signage was required to direct visitors and deliveries accordingly.

Following site visits with the client, a photo audit was undertaken to help define visitor journeys and establish wayfinding principles, working closely with the architecture.

1.4

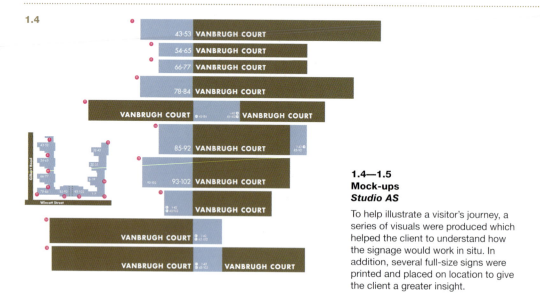

## 1.4—1.5
## Mock-ups
### *Studio AS*

To help illustrate a visitor's journey, a series of visuals were produced which helped the client to understand how the signage would work in situ. In addition, several full-size signs were printed and placed on location to give the client a greater insight.

1.5

1.6

**Futura**
Designed by Paul Renner in 1924–26. Futura is a subtly crafted geometric sansserif, the stroke appears to be unmodulated, but in fact it is carefully shaped to give optical balance.

ABCDEFGHIJKLMNOPQRSTUVWXYZ
abcdefghijklmnopqrstuvwxyz
1234567890?!%"\£&*

VANBRUGH COURT

VANBRUGH COURT

**1.6**
**Design development**
*Studio AS*

A simple colour palette evolved to contrast with the brutal 1970s architecture. Legibility under various lighting conditions was reviewed before the final production and installation.

**Research can be a complicated process, but choosing the right methods will ensure that you have the results you need, and help you avoid undertaking tasks that will not add value to your design work.**

Broadly, research methods can be broken down into three distinct categories:

**Primary research** is new work generated by you during your investigations.

**Secondary research** includes investigation into ideas and processes already conceived and implemented by others.

**Tertiary research** is the summation, or review, of a body of secondary research.

Research cannot be thought of as separate to the design process – the two should inform one another as your project grows. You will need to think in broad terms when starting out and may use secondary and primary techniques, but when refining your designs you are likely to need more direct and pointed techniques such as questionnaires and surveys.

The following pages look at the different types of research that you can employ throughout your design projects and introduces key terminology used to describe them.

**1.7—1.9**
**Sketchbooks**
***Castro Smith* (a student of the University of Gloucestershire, UK)**

The sketchbook is a basic way of recording research, inspiration and ephemera. Shown here are examples by Castro Smith, demonstrating the rich tapestry of thoughts that can be generated through sketching. Rather than drawing from real life, Castro's work is drawn from a mix of imagination, memory and experience, creating a series of surreal worlds, rich in narrative and thought. 'I tend not to plan drawings, I jump straight into it and change the idea of the drawing as it unfolds to me – I imagine stories and worlds and combine it with what I know.'

# Research is formalized curiosity. It is poking and prying with a purpose.

Zora Neale Hurston

1.7

1.8

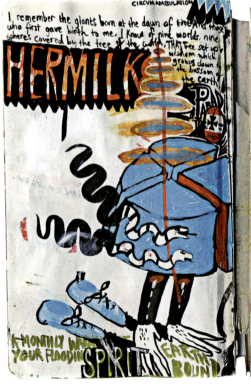

1.9

## Primary research

Primary research describes anything undertaken and generated by you, firsthand. Essentially, it is the development of new knowledge. It is an active process that can range from taking photographs of locations, to drawings of concepts. Sketching is the most immediate way to record information or ideas effectively and is a skill that should be constantly developed.

Primary research can also involve experiments with materials and processes. For example, you might research the durability of materials for a product that will be used outside by setting up tests on the different possibilities, and pitching them against each other in a way that can be tracked. Primary research of this sort will arm you with evidence you can present to your client, to justify your choice of materials.

Primary audience research methods include surveys, interviews and questionnaires, or simply observing people in the environment. This can be conducted with materials ranging from a pen and paper, to cameras or camcorders.

Primary research is often the best way to start working on a project, as it is active and involves you moving quickly and plotting out initial ideas.

## Secondary research

Secondary research involves looking at work that has already been conducted by others. This is helpful, as it can cut down the amount of primary research you need to undertake. Secondary research usually takes place once you've conducted some preliminary experiments and have rough design concepts planned out, or if you have looked at an overview of the subject and wish to focus on one aspect in more detail.

**Data resources**
A data resource is the body of knowledge or information associated with a company or organization. As many companies and organizations are spread over several locations, the data resource is usually held centrally to ensure continuity between operations.

Libraries are a rich source for secondary research – from journals, magazines, books and newspapers, you will find information on a huge variety of subjects. You may also be able to access online <u>data resources,</u> or PDF or web versions of texts that are rare or in demand.

The Internet is another good source of secondary research as it is now the definitive platform for advertising, promotion and disseminating public information. An Internet search on any subject will reveal a number of relevant websites, but use careful discrimination when selecting sources – anyone can update a website with information, but this does not mean it is factual. Only use sources that you know to be reputable, such as government websites, or those linked with longstanding or well-known publications.

## Tertiary research

Tertiary research is where an author has taken several existing pieces of research conducted by others and synthesized them into a review of the subject area – essentially it is many points of research, simplified and contained in a single source. This type of information can be found in magazine or journal reviews and features, encyclopaedias and reference books. In these you might look for reviews of items, theories, processes and design works.

Comparison and review articles that give an overview of specific areas or materials can be particularly valuable. These help cut down the amount of testing you have to conduct, as experts have already considered the effectiveness and potential use of many materials.

1.10

1.11

1.12

**1.10—1.12**
**Primary, secondary and tertiary research**

Primary research is anything undertaken by you, including interviews, questionnaires and surveys. In contrast, secondary research relies on studies and surveys that have already been carried out. Tertiary research is the collection of lots of sets of secondary research, brought together to form a summary or conclusion.

**1.13**

**1.13**
**The Incredible Journey**
*Alicia Waters, Monkey Ink Design*

A constant process of visual research informs Alicia's work. 'I was trying out a new style of drawing people, trying to keep my lines simple yet intriguing. Many of the pieces I do are inspired by people in my life and this was based on my boyfriend and I.'

**1.14**
**Cricket**
*Alicia Waters, Monkey Ink Design*

This textile design was lightly based on combining horse motifs and chevrons.

**1.15–1.16**
**Christmas Vacation Wrapping paper**
*Alicia Waters, Monkey Ink Design*

This festive wrapping paper was created during a Thanksgiving break. 'The research involved me making lists of scenes and narrowing down which parts would be easily recognizable, then fitting them all together like a puzzle.'

**1.14**

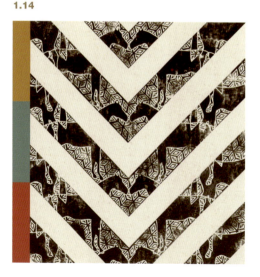

**1.15**

**In addition to the broad categories of primary, secondary and tertiary, there are a number of other key terms used in relation to research that you should become familiar with.**

Constantly questioning, challenging and testing the elements that make up the design process, and being able to describe your investigative work and findings, is key to successful research.

You may choose to look at solutions by analysing hard facts and numbers (quantitative methods – usually gained from questionnaires or tests). You may also use descriptive responses (qualitative research – where a designer or members of a test audience describe their responses to a design). Analytical and propositional research methods will encourage you to pick apart the problem and seek new innovative solutions.

**1.18**

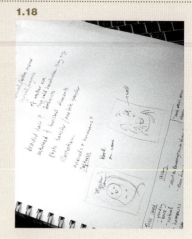

**1.17**

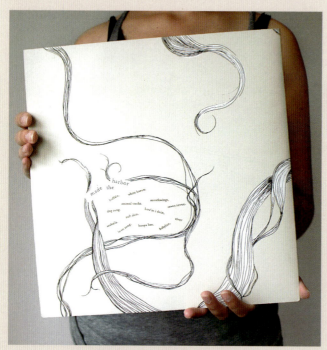

**1.17—1.19**
**Mountain Man band identity and vinyl record**
*Emily Hale*

The band Mountain Man is a group of three women who create music through *a cappella* harmonies. Emily Hale explains how she devised the artwork for their debut album. 'At times when they perform they hold hands to better synchronize, so it seemed appropriate for their album to be covered in intertwining waves of hair. Mountain Man's sound is organic and has a strong and innately feminine quality about it, the hair is intended to mimic just that. The typography for their brand was created by hand – fragile, thin, and wavering, yet grounded by serifs. The poster and vinyl album were both created through the use of silk-screening.'

1.19

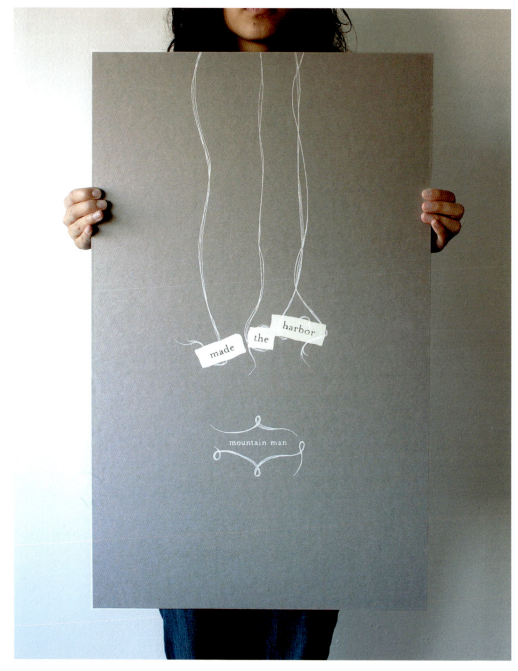

## Quantitative and qualitative research

Quantitative and qualitative research methods are different approaches that both give an insight into your audience. They involve creating a form, survey or questionnaire for a selected audience group to complete. You should design the forms to ensure that they gather all the information that you may need at a later date. Additional information you can ask for may include the participants' age, race, gender and other socio-economic information. This will help you structure your conclusions later on and form meaningful plans.

To undertake quantitative research you would usually ask 'closed' questions, generally only allowing yes or no answers, or giving participants a limited choice (a, b, or c).

Did you enjoy your vacation? ☑ Yes ☐ No

These answers can be counted to indicate the most popular results, and easily converted into statistics. However, it is important that candidates are carefully picked for the survey and members of the intended audience should be consulted first. If a cross-section of the public is required, this must be a true cross-section, not just your colleagues or friends.

Qualitative research involves asking members of the target audience for their opinions on your work, using more 'open' questions. You can ask leading questions that establish why a person feels a certain way, and then enquire what could be done to make their opinions more favourable. Qualitative research questions may relate to the look, feel and understanding of the piece. A summary can be made of the responses and this will form the basis of your action plan.

Did you enjoy your vacation?

Yes I did because we went to the beach.

These two areas can overlap, as it is likely that a survey based on quantitative methods will ask for opinion at some point to break the monotony of 'yes' or 'no' responses. Qualitative questioning can also be converted into statistics, as usually the answers can be seen as largely positive or negative, allowing them to be grouped together to form percentages. You may also notice other trends that can be grouped in this way – for instance, a large percentage of the group may think that a colour change would improve your design work and make it more appealing.

## Descriptive research

Descriptive research methods are used to investigate characteristics and data associated with the area you are studying. This is a process through which you determine who or what you are researching and use quantitative and qualitative methods to source this information. You may wish to use techniques such as trendspotting or coolhunting (see page 117) – the result of this type of investigation will be qualitative. You can also discover quantitative results by looking for patterns and numbers – how many people went into the shop, and what did they look at?

By engaging in descriptive research you will interact with your audience and can ask for comments on possible design solutions, as well as a response to your design work.

Once you have identified your audience, you may ask which solutions they see as most appropriate (see crowdsourcing, page 118), and use this as the basis of your design. You may also simply observe your audience and take note of how they interact with your design, or with similar design pieces (see participant and non-participant observation, page 97).

**Statistics**

Statistics refers to the collection, analysis and interpretation of numerical data. When using statistics, it is vital to show the full picture and not just take parts of the data out of context. Statistics can be manipulated in this way in an attempt to strengthen weak arguments, which has led to it being viewed with scepticism by some.

## Propositional research

Propositional research works by offering alternatives to what already exists; this is of most use when you want to create work that will be different from what is already out there. This is difficult, as you will have to confound the expectations of the audience and present something original to them that does not relate to their current experience.

To do this effectively is a challenge, as we are all influenced, on a conscious or unconscious level, by what we see around us. To break away from this and create something different and truly innovative can be a daunting task. There are devices that can be used to help you consider more extreme options, such as flash cards or lateral thinking exercises. These act as prompts that will provide reference points that can later be rationalized and formed into a solution for the brief.

Propositional questioning is often developed through 'pure research'; this is research conducted without the constraints of commerce, normally by postgraduate students and researchers. When the need to make a project viable and cost effective is not the foremost consideration, the designer can truly innovate. As this new knowledge reaches the design world, it is often applied to more commercial concerns and turned into a product.

**Lateral thinking**

The term 'lateral thinking' was coined by Edward de Bono in the 1960s. It is a means of problem solving that uses creative thinking, rather than established logic. Lateral thinking exercises often encourage you to look at something from a new angle in order to inspire creative and original ideas and solutions.

It is better to have enough ideas for some of them to be wrong, than to be always right by having no ideas at all.

Edward de Bono

**Analytical research**

Analytical research essentially involves taking something apart to see how it works. You can deconstruct a piece of design in terms of its physical structure or its graphic elements.

To take apart a physical artefact, you may look into what powers it, or what makes it work in terms of function. You can learn from this and gain knowledge of how you can make your own designs work.

When looking at any type of design, it is useful to consider how the elements work together and interact with each other. As soon as you place an image or logotype next to typography and introduce colour, a shared meaning will evolve that is greater than the sum of its parts.

A piece of design such as an advertisement or brand identity can be harder to pick to pieces. You will need to consider how the audience interacts with it on a far deeper level – you can use semiotics to do this. Knowledge of semiotics will help you understand the relationship between the object and viewer, as well as how the information is transferred and, through this, how meaning is gained. This is looked at in more detail on pages 60–63.

Many highly intelligent people are poor thinkers. Many people of average intelligence are skilled thinkers. The power of a car is separate from the way the car is driven.

Edward de Bono

**Studio interview:**

**Emily Hale**

Emily Hale, originally from Los Angeles, is a graduate of the Pratt Institute, and now runs a design studio in New York. Her work utilizes illustration in addition to graphic design, and includes everything from eco-friendly packaging designs to album covers.

## What does research mean to you?

Research is the very foundation of my entire design process. It enables me to understand what the design challenge is, what the problem is, or what the question is that I am trying to answer through my design. If you have no idea what you are trying to solve or create, your solution won't be relevant or appropriate.

## Where do you start with a brief?

I first like to sit with a brief for a moment and read it a couple of times. I then write, sketch, and summarize my first thoughts on paper, push them aside, and jump into research. I analyse my initial ideas after I've done the research. Often, the research leads me elsewhere, but I find that initial purging of thoughts to be quite useful.

## What methods of research do you find to be most effective?

I've found the most effective forms of research to be the ones that get you the closest to your direct source. Meaning that you are either interviewing people at a location, experimenting with a material, or even going to an event that's relevant to your project. The closer you can get to your subject matter, the stronger and more thoughtful your solution will be.

## Where do you find inspiration?

I find the most inspiration through just talking with as wide a variety of people as possible. People who aren't necessarily in design – people who are 75 years old and have a lifetime's worth of amazing experiences to learn from; people who are from a different country; or people who are in a field that you know nothing about. Each person holds a unique perspective and when you are open to that, the knowledge you gain is the most inspiring thing.

**1.20**
**Does the Type of Disaster Change What Matters?**
Editorial pitch for *New York Times* magazine, analysing how different disasters affect which items people see as important. The story is a very personal one, involving a series of interviews looking at the objects people chose to save in the event of a disaster. 'In all instances of actual disasters people had encountered, it seemed that what connected them all was the desire to bring sentimental items; the idea of sentimentality being above practicality, when faced with the prospect of losing everything.'

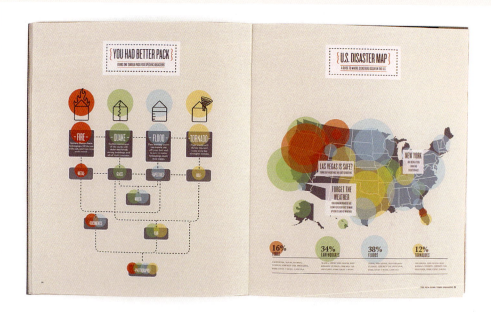

1.20

**You have been asked to create a new brand for a company which aims to engage socially active teenagers in new and different ways. They want to design and promote a range of smartphones that are customizable, affordable, and technologically advanced enough to compete with established brands. They aim to communicate with their audience in an informal and direct way.**

**Brief**

Using only a pen and paper, consider the different research methods and techniques that might be employed to gain the information needed to understand the audience and assess the best approach. As a starting point, consider the following:

- Will you speak to members of the intended audience, and if so how will you identify and approach them?

- Would questionnaires or surveys be more effective?

- What secondary research can be undertaken, and where can this information be found?

- How you will identify and research rival brands?

- What information can you take from this research and how might it be used to inform your project?

**Project objective**

- To consider the steps of research needed to work in the most informed and productive way.

**Recommended reading related to this project**

Barry, P (2008). *The Advertising Concept Book: Think Now, Design Later.* Thames & Hudson

Burtenshaw, K et al. (2011). *The Fundamentals of Creative Advertising.* AVA Publishing

Clarke, M (2007). *Verbalising the Visual: Translating Art and Design into Words.* AVA Publishing

Stephenson, K and Hampshire, M (2007). *Packaging: Design Successful Packaging for Specific Customer Groups.* Rotovision

Stone, T (2010). *Managing the Design Process, Volume 1: Concept Development.* Rockport Publishers

Wigan, M (2006). *Basics Illustration: Thinking Visually.* AVA Publishing

**Chapter 2 – Understanding context**

**In this chapter we look at how different contexts surrounding a design project can play a crucial part in research considerations, as well as informing the development of solutions.**

From audience and social contexts such as demographics and politics, to design contexts such as aesthetics and trends, we look at how context affects the ways in which your work is developed and, eventually, received. Key terminology that will help you to classify and describe this information is also explored.

**At any point in time, there will be factors external to your projects that will profoundly affect how they are received. Investigating these is crucial to understanding the social implications of where your design will be seen, and how it will be understood.**

Social and cultural context must be understood clearly to ensure that your work is effective and clearly targeted. Many products have failed because the designer and manufacturer did not fully consider the wider picture and possible connotations for different groups of people.

Any change in society can greatly alter how a piece of design is understood, as the audience brings with them a different set of experiences and cultural connotations. These affect whether a person enjoys and buys into your concepts. Perception is a difficult thing to control as there are so many external factors, but broadly understanding different social, political and economic contexts will help you to achieve this.

### Economics

The most delicate and potentially limiting matter in terms of design is often the economic climate. Economics can affect everything from the production and sourcing of materials, to the labour force that will eventually realize your designs.

Trade is one of the most prominent concerns for designers and clients, whether launching a new product, enhancing the standing of an established brand, or working on a self-initiated project. Put simply, we need money to make things, and consumers need money to buy them. If a company is struggling financially, design budgets will often be cut back. This is not wholly negative, as more innovative and cost-effective solutions, such as viral and social media campaigns, can be used without large financial investments.

Strong research into current financial issues will help you to succeed with things such as business plans and loans that are often vital when you want to start a freelance career or practice of your own.

**2.1
Poster for Leeds Design for Activism Festival
*Merlin Mason***

This poster pays homage to the *First Things First* manifesto published by Ken Garland in 1964, and more specifically to the second edition released in 2000. The reference is clear; designers need to consider their actions and the types of companies they sell their services to.

In addition to some of the year 2000 themes, Merlin added greenwashing – the practice of companies promoting themselves as being green with little proof that they are. 'At the time, Climate Camp protests were very current in people's minds.'

A valuable part of your research should be to question and challenge the credentials of potential employers, so you have a clear brief and, ultimately, a clear conscience.

# Engagé:
# Design for ~~Dog Biscuits~~
~~Diamonds~~
~~Detergents~~
~~Hair Gel~~
~~Greenwash~~
~~Cigarettes~~
~~Credit Cards~~
~~Sneakers~~
~~Butt Toners~~
~~Light Beer~~
# Activism

**Engagé: Design for Activism Exhibition**
**Thurs July 2 — Sat July 4 2009**
**www.designactivism.org**

A student/graduate exhibition that explores the role
of design as a tool for activism and social change.
**Part of the Leeds Festival of Design Activism.**

2.1

## Local to global

The global community is now closer to being a reality than ever before. Thanks to the Internet, it is now possible for a client and designer relationship to span different continents. This is positive in many ways as it means there is a far larger pool of jobs to apply for, but it also means there is more competition for each job and new challenges to face.

As any given designer will now deal with a very diverse range of clients, your knowledge of each client's environment and culture is key to getting the job right. Each culture brings with it its own specific contexts that need to be understood in order to make sure that you are creating work that is accessible and appropriate.

It is equally important to have a good understanding of the local contexts in which you work as these are in a constant state of flux. Populations can shift dramatically over the course of a few years, particularly as immigration and travel are now more commonplace. Any city centre can be seen as a vibrant cultural experience in which cultural identities are mixed and merge into something new.

**Global village**
In his 1962 book, *The Gutenberg Galaxy: The Making of Typographic Man,* Marshall McLuhan proposed the idea of a connected 'global community'. Predicting the invention of the Internet, this term is now often used to describe the world wide web.

The next medium, whatever it is – it may be the extension of consciousness – will include television as its content, not as its environment, and will transform television into an art form.

Marshall McLuhan

2.2

**2.2—2.3**
**Frozen Yogurt**
*Luciano Ferreira*

Local vernacular is used in this packaging study project, linking the product to the intended user. The references to local typographic styles give the packaging an important differentiating factor.

2.3

41

## Identity and intersections

A person can define their identity in a number of ways, including official <u>demographic</u> definitions such as profession or gender, and personal ones that may refer to their hobbies and interests. The most obvious areas we divide people into can also be the most useful – they include age, race and gender. It is important to know which group of people you are targeting with your design work, and to speak to this group during your research. The sections of the public you may want to speak to might be as broad as males, or as specific as Afro-Caribbean women aged between 24 and 40 living in London. The reason for this grouping is to ensure you have a clear idea who will buy your product or service and can create design work aimed specifically at them. In terms of productivity, it is important that you define this audience early on to avoid wasting time researching and interviewing the wrong people.

As culture is ever changing and many more sub-cultures appear each year, the way people define themselves changes too. It is therefore important to keep up to date with cultural developments and know how people group themselves in informal ways. A product you are designing may have an audience that cannot be easily defined in terms of age or gender, but can be defined through common likes and buying choices. For example, a technological product concerned with web development may be aimed at designers of both genders and all ages and races; the audience is arrived at here because of the product's use, but also due to the fact this group would want to align themselves with up-to-the-minute products to stay on top of new developments.

**Demographic**
A group or a market segment of an audience, often defined by shared characteristics, for example age, gender, interests, income or buying patterns.

2.4

**2.4—2.5**
**Fleming & Howland**
*Gavin Ambrose/Xavier Young*

These adverts use room sets and styling appropriate for the magazines they appear in. Demographic factors such as the gender and economic profiles of the magazines' readers are taken into account when selecting where and how to place advertising. What is right for one market isn't necessarily right for another.

2.5

**2.6**

**Vernacular**
Vernacular, in the context of graphic design, refers to the visual language and symbols that surround us, especially in a particular location or culture. Famous examples include Barry Deck's typeface Template Gothic, that was based on the signage of a local launderette.

**2.6—2.9**
**SkimBeam**
*Fuse Collective*

Shown are skim boards with graphics by Fuse Collective. The users of any given product form a demographic – linked by their values, interests and aesthetic preferences. These shared values manifest themselves into a <u>vernacular</u>, or visual language. This visual language may be appropriate to one demographic, but not to another, so having a clear understanding of who you are aiming at is critically important.

**2.7**

2.8

2.9

## Politics

Politics can play a major part in the creation and development of new design work, and can also affect access to research and funding sources, such as grants from arts bodies. If there are nationwide political and financial concerns, the arts are unfortunately the first thing to suffer and therefore support will be far harder to come by.

Many great graphic design campaigns and images have been directly inspired by political matters, from the Great War posters from both the East and the West, to advertising agency Saatchi and Saatchi's work with the UK Conservative party in the 1980s. Another example of this is the *First Things First* manifesto created by Ken Garland and first published in 1964, before being updated in 2000. This highlighted social concerns and encouraged designers to lend their talents to causes, as well as commercial enterprises.

Ethics is one of the most vital concerns faced by designers and political understanding is essential in helping you navigate this. Green politics will be at the forefront of decisions made by many clients. There are implications such as choosing to use local, Fairtrade or recycled materials. A clear consideration of ethics could make or break a product or service – if a client operates in a 'green' and ethical way this can have a real impact on how they are perceived by their audience. Many companies, regardless of the type of business, will want to demonstrate consideration for the environment as consumers see this as a real positive.

Ethical concerns should not be viewed as negative or constrictive as they can add value to a piece of work. The population as a whole is increasingly aware of ethical concerns, so if you can state that your goods are ethical, your designs will be that much more attractive.

**Green politics**
A political ideology based around environmental consideration and ecological sustainability. Green parties are now present in many countries around the world and tend to be especially prominent in Western societies.

2.10

**2.10**
**Hemp 4 Haiti Project**
*Blake Lowther* **(a student at Portfolio Center, USA)**

This packaging design shows a creative reinterpretation of an old idea. The exterior packaging of these relief products is made from sustainable hemp. This can be unravelled and used as twine once the product has been used. The inspiration for this came from an unlikely place, as Blake explains: 'The idea was inspired by the Great Depression. Flour sacks would be printed with a pattern. After the flour was gone, the women would use the old flour sacks and turn them into skirts or shirts.'

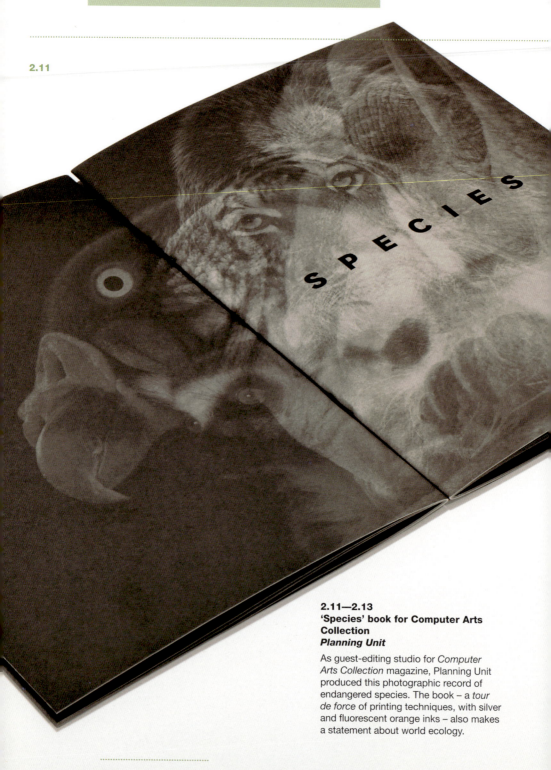

**2.11—2.13**
**'Species' book for Computer Arts Collection**
*Planning Unit*

As guest-editing studio for *Computer Arts Collection* magazine, Planning Unit produced this photographic record of endangered species. The book – a *tour de force* of printing techniques, with silver and fluorescent orange inks – also makes a statement about world ecology.

2.12

2.13

**Knowledge and understanding of contexts should extend to those around design itself, as well as audience and social factors. While design is intrinsically linked to culture as a whole, there are specific contexts, such as the history of certain art movements and the way styles and trends are cultivated, that need to be understood and taken into consideration.**

To understand design contexts, looking back is as essential as pushing the possibilities of the discipline. All design carries baggage through the use of type, imagery and material that the audience understands and relates to.

**Avant-garde**
The term avant-garde refers to work that is new, experimental, innovative, or simply ahead of its time – things that go against the established norm.

### Historical context

Understanding what has come before will help you to see where we are now, and where culture and design might go next. To get a broad overview of design history you should investigate the cultural and historical events that have shaped it. A thorough understanding of these will show you the context in which design exists and will reveal its lineage.

Many art and design movements have had a long lasting effect on graphic design. We now briefly describe some of these key movements and the key players – use this as a starting point for your own research into historical contexts.

**The Arts and Crafts Movement** started in England in the 1860s, bringing about heightened interest in traditional crafts, partly as a reaction against the industrial age. At the same time in France, **Impressionism** was developed, challenging classical understanding of painting by focusing on light and open compositions. This led to movements such as **pointillism** and **art nouveau**, both with associated literature and philosophies. These styles were reflected in the work of designers such as Henri de Toulouse-Lautrec and Aubrey Beardsley, both of whom are still hugely popular and inspirational today.

Around this time in the former Soviet Union, the <u>**avant-garde**</u> movement ushered in a new way of thinking about design, leading to **constructivism**. This is still hugely influential and has inspired designers such as Neville Brody.

**Futurism** developed after the First World War and looked to a bright future, rather than looking to the past. This optimism faded with the advent of the Second World War.

**Modernism** continued the revolt against the art world that the avant-garde and Impressionists began. Modernists sought to re-shape and improve their surroundings and create new works. A lot of design created at this time sought to highlight the materials used.

**Postmodernism** began as a reaction to modernism and rejected many of its ideas. Postmodernism is not a particular style, as such, rather an overall idea. This way of thinking rejects the strict rational and superficial processes employed in modernism and encourages a return to the decoration and expression of earlier movements, but it does so in a knowing way, often employing wit or irony.

**2.14**
**Cabbage and Vine tapestry, 1879**
*William Morris*

**2.15**
**Puppy, Bilbao, 1992**
*Jeff Koons*

Having an awareness of the past can inform your research and design practice. From classic examples of design, through to contemporary art and literature – the potential sources of influence and reference are vast.

**2.14**

**2.15**

## Aesthetics

Aesthetics deals with the appreciation of how things look, and what people understand from this. It is a judgement of style or taste and describes the appeal of an object or design. The term itself is rooted in the psychological study of how people respond to beauty and art. It can be argued that the beauty, or aesthetic value, of an object is held within the object itself. However, many people view judgements on this to be rooted inside the viewer through the feelings and experiences that they bring to the work.

It is often used to describe the beauty or style of a design – something may be described as having a 'modernist aesthetic', which would mean that it adheres to the values of the modernist movement.

Aesthetic considerations are important as these are what a viewer will first be attracted to, but this surface value should be backed up with a good understanding of the audience and a strong idea. Good research will help you to determine the aesthetic values that you should employ to ensure that your audience responds to your work in the way that you intended. If judged correctly, the message and intention of the work should sit comfortably alongside this.

### Tribal art

A broad genre of art, objects and outdoor constructions created by people living in tribal societies. Its purpose is often religious or ceremonial. Tribal images, masks and statues are not made according to the laws of perspective.

**2.16**
**Flora and Fauna**
*Lynnie Zulu*

Lynnie Zulu's portraits focus on tribal art forms revisited with a modern aesthetic. 'The research I undertake usually stems from tribal and cultural perspectives. This inspires the raw and mysterious content that is so important in my work. I tend to revisit artists or illustrators whose work is very different to mine for inspiration. I find their different techniques and approaches very refreshing, and it pushes me further,' explains Lynnie.

# Art is the imposing of a pattern on experience, and our aesthetic enjoyment is recognition of the pattern.

Alfred North Whitehead

2.16

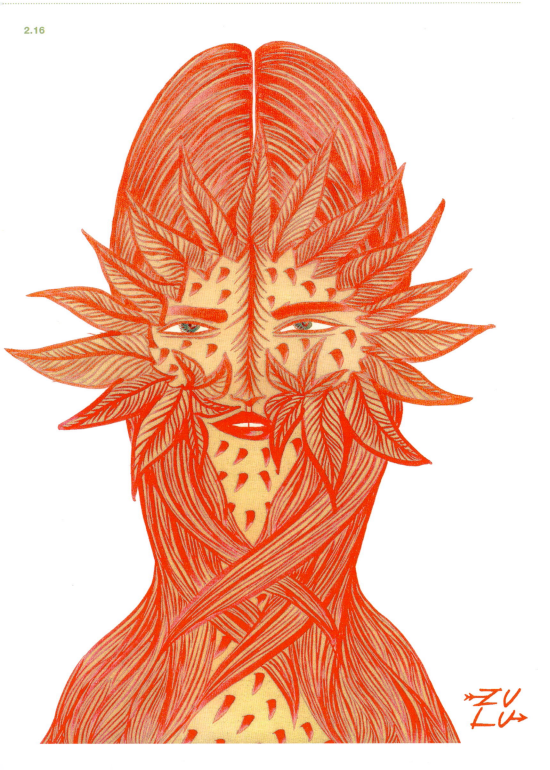

## Style

Style can refer to the appearance, design and construction of a given object or design. The terms style and trend can be seen as interchangeable, but a style is longer lasting and more over-arching than a trend and can be associated with an individual person, product or brand. A style may incorporate many different trends and aesthetic values; and it will develop over time.

A style becomes a way of doing things. For example, 'modernism' and 'grunge' are kinds of typography that have their own appeal and are commonly used, but neither is particularly reliant on fashion, as they are established styles.

The style of any design produced should always be reliant on identification and knowledge of the audience. As styles are generally well recognized, it is useful to look into these associations when creating work as they can carry much of the meaning. A stylistic choice can signal important information to the audience.

**2.17**
**Typefaces**

Typefaces are a reflection of the styles and artistic concerns of the time in which they were produced. Univers, designed by Adrian Frutiger in 1954, consists of 44 faces with 16 uniquely numbered weights. This approach was in keeping with modernist themes. This font was designed to be the only typeface a designer would need, being suitable for any use.

Later developments in computer technology have allowed for the creation of ever more experimental and transient typefaces.

**2.17**

Univers – a typeface in the modernist style.

Other typefaces take influence from themes of fashion, for example grunge.

Many graphic designers have their own distinctive style and it will be this that attracts clients. For new designers starting out, it is important that this style does not rely on current trends or their work will quickly look dated.

2.18

2.19

Over time, styles change, partly in reaction to previous styles and partly in response to new technology. Peter Paul Rubens's view of the female nude, for example, was influenced by the times he lived in – and fashions have changed. Technology continues to have an influence on typographic style, and even changes the way language is constructed.

**2.18**
**Venus at the Mirror, 1615**
*Peter Paul Rubens*

Perceptions of beauty, taste and aesthetics change over time.

**2.19**
**Emoticons**

All art, high and low, is subject to the fashions and prevailing styles and trends of the time. The way we view our surroundings, and what we consider the 'norm', is a construct of this environment.

**2.20**
**Ten Principles of Good Design**
*Dieter Rams*

German industrial designer Dieter Rams created these 'Ten principles of good design' to try to extend beyond the 'trap' of style.

2.20

| 1 | Is innovative |
|---|---|
| 2 | Makes a product useful |
| 3 | Is aesthetic |
| 4 | Makes a product understandable |
| 5 | Is unobtrusive |
| 6 | Is honest |
| 7 | Is long-lasting |
| 8 | Is thorough down to the last detail |
| 9 | Is environmentally friendly |
| 10 | Is as little design as possible |

## Trends and technology

A trend is a style or fashion that is current and often short-lived. It is important to keep up to date with trends in design, technology, art and fashion as these all influence culture as a whole and, through this, design. The ability to identify trends is key to creating work that is current.

Technology makes it easier than ever to keep up with developments in the arts. Websites have become more complex, faster, and more dynamic. Blogs allow you to track new work and designers, as well as changes in the ways ideas are realized. Social media sites allow designers to engage with one another in debate and share ideas, regardless of where in the world they are. There are also trend prediction sites that help you find things that are on the cusp of happening. This ease and speed of access to new work means that the lifespan of trends is now shorter than ever, as the audience and creators of new work are always looking for what is next.

In 1937, author and art historian James Laver proposed a timetable for the cycle of fashion. Published in *Taste and Fashion*, it is tongue-in-cheek, but Laver had importantly identified that there is a predictable cycle to fashion.

2.23

**2.22**

| Indecent | Ten years before its time |
|----------|---------------------------|
| Shameless | Five years before its time |
| Outré (Daring) | One year before its time |
| Smart | 'Current fashion' |
| Dowdy | One year after its time |
| Hideous | Ten years after its time |
| Ridiculous | 20 years after its time |
| Amusing | 30 years after its time |
| Quaint | 50 years after its time |
| Charming | 70 years after its time |
| Romantic | 100 years after its time |
| Beautiful | 150 years after its time |

**2.21**
**The Montreal Biosphere**
*Richard Buckminster Fuller*

Fuller's 1967 building at Parc Jean-Drapeau is a museum dedicated to the environment. The geodesic dome, which Fuller invented, is essentially a self-supporting structure.

**2.22**
**The fashion cycle**
*James Laver*

Laver's fashion cycle aims to consolidate the changes of trends into a simple timetable.

**2.23**
**The Segway Personal Transporter**
*Dean Kamen*

Trends come and trends go. The Segway Personal Transporter (PT) – a passing trend, or the future of transport?

2.24

**2.24—2.26**
**Deformable cover for *Novum***
**magazine**
***Paperlux***

German design studio Paperlux
created this unique deformable cover
for the November 2011 issue of
*Novum* magazine. It was an elaborate
print job that included six different
colour schemes after 48,000 print
passes with 140 punch cuts per issue.

The resulting cover, inspired by
the ideas and concepts of Richard
Buckminster Fuller, is pliable along its
cuts within the grid of the geometric
design, inviting play and interaction.

2.25

2.26

**Graphic design education and research has sought to generate new knowledge and understanding of relevant theories, many of which are now widely accepted as being ideas that all artists and designers should be familiar with.**

Understanding relevant theories and concepts is key for the practice-based designer, as it can introduce you to research opportunities that go far beyond the obvious.

**Semiotics**

Semiotics is one of the most widely used theoretical perspectives within design as it attempts to explain how people read the visual language we develop. The study of semiotics was first undertaken by linguist Ferdinand de Saussure, who studied the development of words and how they relate to objects or concepts. He coined the following terms, commonly used by designers to describe the relationship between image and message:

*Signs* Each sign is made of a signifier (a sound, written word or image) and the signified (the concept or meaning).

*Signifiers* Words or phrases that can be seen as arbitrary, yet express meaning to people within a shared culture. There is no explicit connection between the signifier and its meaning – this has to be learned. For example, every language has a different word for 'bear', but the speakers of each language learn to relate the word to the object.

**Ferdinand de Saussure**
Ferdinand de Saussure (1857–1913) was an influential Swiss linguist. He proposed that language is a structured system of signs and symbols. His principles became the foundation for semiotics, which has been used extensively in critical and cultural studies since the late 1960s.

The transference of culture in time can, in large measure, be described as the conservation of sign systems serving as a control on behaviour.

Doris Bradbury

**2.27**

Charles Sanders Peirce (1839–1914) developed the theory of three kinds of signs, also used in semiotics:

*Icon* A graphic image that directly resembles what it represents. For instance, an illustration of a horse is an icon of a horse, as it directly resembles the animal.

*Index* A sign that only makes sense when its context is taken into consideration. For example, a road sign with a symbol that only has meaning because of its placement next to the road.

*Symbol* A symbol has an arbitrary relationship with the object or concept it signifies – a symbol of a heart has no direct relationship to the concept of love, but it is generally accepted that these two things are connected.

Roland Barthes (1915–1980) was a more recent influential figure in semiotics. He defined the following terms:

*Convention* An agreement specific to a group or culture that a sign represents a particular thing, object or concept. This can be a sign that is understood worldwide, such as the Red Cross identity, or a sign that is far more specific, like the crest on a football shirt.

*Denotation* The surface or literal meaning of a sign, removed from any context. An example of this might be a sign that reads 'Danger!'. The sign means nothing more than danger, but the user will determine exactly what the danger is by judging the context in which the sign is seen.

*Connotation* The idea or meaning associated with a thing that goes far beyond the literal denotation. An example of this would be a photograph that has been given a sepia tone to create a feeling of nostalgia – the process will add little to the content of the image, but the public as a whole understands that sepia signals age, therefore they react to it accordingly. The enhanced meaning attached to the photograph may be arbitrary, but these values are learnt and agreed upon by most people.

**2.27**
**Icon (a), index (b) and symbol (c)**

Shown above are three images.

The horse *icon* is a direct representation of the horse.

The *indexical* road sign shows an inherent relationship between the signifier (the bumps in the road) and the signified (where those bumps are).

The *symbolic* sign is conventionalized, but shows an arbitrary relationship between the signifier (the heart) and the signified (love).

René Magritte's famous painting of 1928, La Trahison des Images (The Treachery of Images) depicts a painting of a pipe, and underneath it the text, Ceci n'est pas une pipe, or 'This is not a pipe.' This apparent contradiction is of course true, the painting is of a pipe, it is not a pipe. Understanding that images are representations and not objects, is key to understanding semiotics, and understanding how we view images and meanings.

Ceci n'est pas une pipe.

## Studio interview:

### Andrew Hussey

Andrew Hussey completed his studies with a BA (Hons) in Graphic Design from Bath Spa University, in the UK. He works as a freelance design and branding consultant, with clients in the corporate, cultural and education sectors.

### What does research mean to you?

The research stage is a pivotal part of any design project, large or small. For me, it's the opportunity to gain a wider understanding of the brief, the client and the audience, and ensure I'm communicating messages appropriately. It helps me form structured, measurable objectives that I can review and develop later.

### Where do you start with a brief?

I start with an open mind and make sure the brief has my full attention. It's also vital to listen to the client before asking questions and discussing the brief informally. In my experience, successful projects are built on trust and good relationships.

Once I have a good level of background knowledge, I split the brief into primary and secondary objectives. Secondary objectives encompass a broader perspective and longer time-frame, and include considerations such as brand consistency and development.

### What methods of research do you find to be the most effective?

I can't single out one effective research method. It's important to listen to your client's thoughts and findings first, but then trust your instincts. I like to take a hands-on approach to research and try to speak to the end-user, however, it's not always possible. I always draw on my experience, but you have to treat each job differently.

### Where do you find inspiration?

Rightly or wrongly, I don't think I ever switch off. Designers are a different breed in this respect. I'm constantly absorbing communications and visual messages wherever I go. In fact, bad or even un-designed things can often be the seed of an idea.

I also think my day-to-day environment is really important. I think it's vital to surround yourself with things that inspire you.

**2.28**
**Earth Music Bristol**
Andrew had the pleasure of working with St George's Bristol, one of the UK's leading concert halls, to develop a visual identity for a new music festival called Earth Music Bristol. Once the look and feel of the identity was established, Andrew applied it across online and printed communications.

2.28

To design for a particular market you must first understand its current state. By analysing the design that exists within a particular context, you will get to know its conventions and develop a better grasp of the opportunities available. This might mean going with the trends and ideas that currently exist, or rejecting them in favour of something new that will challenge the audience.

**Brief**

For this task you are asked to analyse one particular range of goods in a supermarket from the following list:

- Soap powder

- Canned soup

- Cola

- Biscuits

- Cereal

You may wish to narrow your selection slightly, for example, children's cereal.

Once you have selected a range of goods to look at, analyse the presentation and packaging. You may wish to look at:

- Colour

- Typography and lettering

- Scale

- Material

- The use of imagery

- Intended viewer

Try to identify which characteristics the different products have in common, and which are more unusual, or unique to a particular brand. Which features do you think are the most important or most effective?

**Project objectives**

- Developing primary research skills in a particular context.

- Identifying the traits that work within established brands.

**Recommended reading related to this project**

Barnard, M (2005). *Graphic Design as Communication*. Routledge

Berger, J (2008). *Ways of Seeing.* Penguin Classics

Bergström, B (2008). *Essentials of Visual Communication.* Laurence King Publishing

Goddard, A (2001). *The Language of Advertising*. Routledge

Hall, S (2007). *This Means This, This Means That: A User's Guide to Semiotics*. Laurence King Publishing

McLuhan, M, and Fiore, Q (2008). *The Medium is the Massage: An Inventory of Effects.* Penguin Classics

Sudjic, D (2009). *The Language of Things: Design, Luxury, Fashion, Art: How We Are Seduced by the Objects Around Us*. Penguin

## Chapter 3 – Planning your work

**Being well prepared for research is as important as the research itself. Research should be a reflective and determined process, not a reactive one. Creating a clear plan in the early stages of your project will help you to achieve this.**

Considering which systems you will use to gather, store, categorize and access your research can save valuable time later, when deadlines are looming. In this chapter we look at some of the key elements you should consider from the outset to plan a successful project.

**The brief is the starting point for all design projects, and should contain all of the information you need to successfully plan, research and complete your project.**

A university brief is usually less constrained than an industry brief because an educational project allows room for you to develop your technical and analytical skills without commercial constraints. You will also be given enough time to discover, make mistakes and seek feedback from your tutors and peers. A similar project in industry would happen in a fraction of this time, as you will be expected to be adept and skilled, though you will still gain new skills with each project.

A commercial brief will be set by your client and will usually include details such as intended audience, budget, deadlines and goals for the project. You will often have to interrogate the brief and converse with the client to get the best from the information you are presented with.

Keep in mind that the client setting the brief is usually not the person who will use the finished design – do not confuse your client with your audience. While there is a need to please your client as they are offering the financial motive, you should look to the audience for inspiration and direction – getting this balance right is a great challenge.

In responding to the brief, you should plan ahead and consider which strategies and methods you will employ throughout the project. You should begin by developing your aims and methodology; these should be referred back to throughout the project, as they form the basis of your approach and give you something to measure your progress and success against.

**3.1**
**Stages of research**
This is a simplified diagram of the stages of research, from an initial brief to a solution or outcome.

3.1

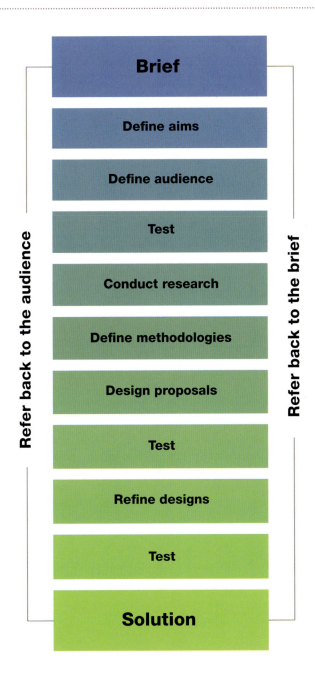

## Aims

The aims of your project are what you want to achieve, or what the brief is asking you to do. It is important that these aims are clearly set out at the beginning of your project and referred to throughout the process, as they form the reason for your investigation as well as providing its direction.

The initial aims may be what the success of the final designs is measured against, but you should not let this inhibit your creativity. Projects often change greatly between the beginning and the end of the creative process. Your client may have an idea of what they want to achieve, but it is your job to find the best way to do this. By working with them, you may be able to offer elements that they have not considered.

From a personal perspective, your aims may include ways to develop your own skills, or even to use the project to gain more work and commissions. Your aims will also develop as you gain a greater understanding of the audience. This may lead you to adjust the brief, or you may find an alternative route to help you achieve your aims more effectively.

## Methodology

Your methodology is the framework for your investigation; the rules, techniques and procedures you plan to use. This may include different methods of acquiring information, and may also refer to relevant theories and concepts that you will use to describe and interpret your results.

To define your methodology you should first consider your field of study – the world in which the finished work will exist, including the audience, existing design and competitors. You can then develop your focus within this, or identify the problem that needs solving and consider which lines of enquiry will be most relevant.

The processes you use should be systematic, logical and predefined, rather than reactive. If you think of research as a cyclical process, it will help you to consider ways through which you can identify your aims and methodologies.

**3.2**
**Harmonie-intérieure**
*Fabien Barral*

Over time, all designers develop different methodologies for working. French designer Fabien Barral explains the unorthodox approach that he adopted as part of the methodology used to create these wonderful interior installations. 'I am the kind of designer that needs to eat thousands and thousands of images before going into the creative phase. Most of the time, I do a moodboard of things I love, and then when I am driving, or walking in the street, or even when I am falling asleep, images and concepts come to my mind.'

3.2

### 3.3—3.5
### Tekël
### *Matthieu Delahaie*

3.3

Produced in collaboration with photographer Marco Dos Santos, this artwork for contemporary band Tekël is intriguing and disturbing in equal measure. Band members and dogs were photographed in the same position under the same light and later morphed using image manipulation software.

The original idea came from the band members who had collated examples of dogs' heads superimposed onto human bodies, and this execution pushes the boundaries of this idea into an eerily realistic result.

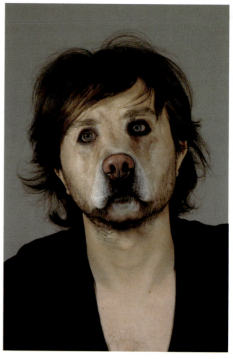

3.4

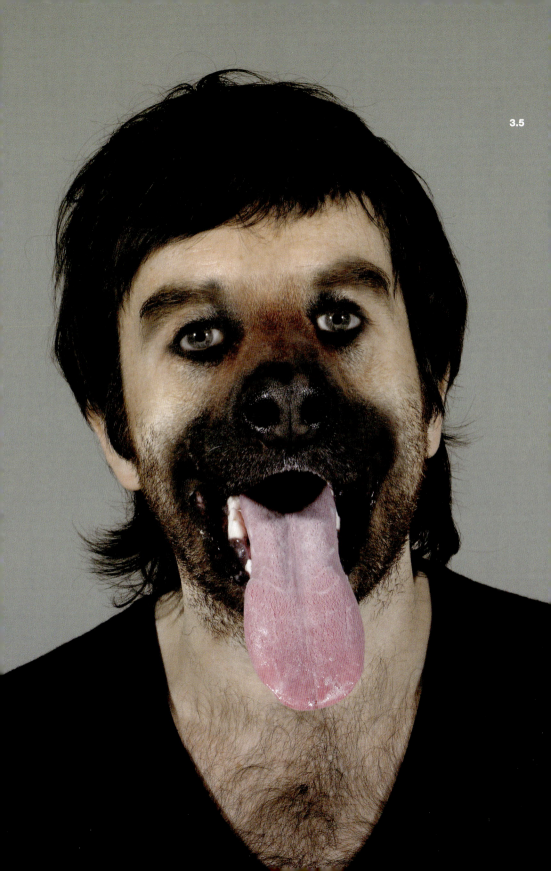

**Perhaps the most crucial information to extract from your project brief is who the target audience is. A large part of the research cycle is spent choosing the right materials, typefaces and colours, but these decisions will only be effective if the audience relates to, and understands them. The importance of audience research cannot be overstated.**

Your audience are the <u>end-users</u> of your product; therefore they are key to the success of your work. Members of your audience make the choice of whether or not to engage with your design solutions. If you know your audience well enough, you can be confident that they will find your results appealing and buy into your designs.

You can define your audience in many different ways. It may be that a product you are designing is aimed at a particular gender, or age group. With most products, you will have to consider the expendable income your audience has – it is no use designing something that they cannot afford. Identifying your audience early on will help you to effectively plan and target your research, and ensure your ideas and designs are as relevant and appealing to them as possible.

To get the best from research into your audience, it is useful to immerse yourself in the places where the finished work will exist. If you are creating work for a retail environment, for example, you could spend time around the shoppers who will engage with the work you are looking to create. Observe their habits, looking with particular attention at how they move around the shop, how they interact with displays and products, how they choose products and eventually make their purchase. You should also consider what other design work they may encounter in this environment; this will give you a good indication of the type of work you may wish to make. All of these factors can inform the nature, placement and content of your work, and this process can be applied to any work that has a specific audience.

**End-user**
An end-user is the person who will be using a product, but there is an interesting caveat to this. The ultimate user of a product isn't necessarily the person who buys it. Many products are bought by women, but used by men; or bought by adults and used by children. Don't assume that your end-user is also your purchaser.

3.6
**The Handkerchief – Robert Adam Architects**
*Webb & Webb*
An example of knowing what you want to say, and who you are saying it to. This tongue in cheek invitation, to 'hard-nosed architects' is playful and engaging, and is clear who its audience is.

When developing a project, the first step is to identify who the end-user will be. Candidates from that audience group are then questioned to determine their feelings about current products or design, and to see how they think improvements could be made. If the audience is allowed to guide the research process in this way, the results will always be appropriate.

Once a product has been developed, audience candidates would be asked to give feedback on how effective the design results are and whether this fits their needs. This testing can take place in a number of different ways – from user experience labs, often employed by web design agencies, to observing people as they interact with a product, or questioning them afterwards. More information about testing can be found on pages 144–147.

**3.6**

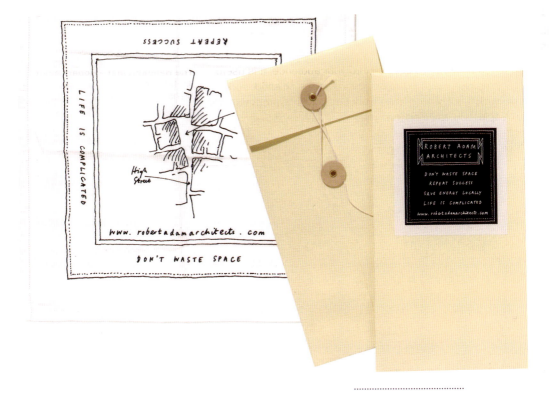

An important consideration before undertaking research for your project is the sources you intend to make use of. The Internet has opened up new ways to source research, but as with all information gathered through research, you must check the credibility of each source carefully.

As it is now possible for anyone to update a website or blog, you need to be able to distinguish fact from opinion. You can do this by looking for some key things. Always check the source of the information – an established newspaper, for example, is far more likely to check their facts than a blogger. Government sources are generally regarded as credible, but you should still look at information from such sources carefully – there may be an agenda, and facts can be manipulated to prove a point they were not intended to.

This should also be considered when speaking to members of your audience. It is important that interviewees are honest in their responses in order to provide credible and valuable insights. It is good practice to ask preliminary questions to determine whether the interviewee has any history with your client, or any reason to supply answers that are incorrect.

**3.7—3.8**
**The Things That Interest You & Me**
*Ally Carter* (a student at the University of Brighton, UK)

Poster series, based on frequently searched terms from Google. The resulting prints question the quality of the information we consume on a daily basis. This mix of modern technology and traditional printing techniques has become a theme of Ally's work. 'I am inspired by the possibilities of older, more traditional printing techniques and employing them when they are contextually relevant to a project. Despite always starting with an idea as the basis, both practical techniques and research then tend to feed off each other throughout the course of the design process.'

3.7

BAGGAGE

BJECT TO

NEMENT

POSED

RICTIONS!

LOWER YOUR CALORIE INTAKE

**WITHOUT**
**STARVING.**
ONLY EAT
**BREAKFAST,**
**LUNCH**
AND
**DINNER**

THERE'S
NOTHING WRONG
WITH
**YOU**
FOR A WOMAN TO ORGASM IS NOT
NOT AS EASY OR MECHANICAL AS
IT IS FOR A MAN.

JUSTIN BIEBER
IS RESIDING
IN
BUCKHEAD
ATLANTA
GEORGIA
IN
THE
USA

**FML**
COLLOQUIAL
ACRONYM
FOR
**FUCK**
**MY LIFE**

# THE COTSWOLDS
### ARE A
## RANGE OF HILLS
### IN
## WEST-CENTRAL
## ENGLAND.

HE'S CHEATING ON YOU
AFRAID OF BEING TIED DOWN
THINKS YOU ARE AFTER
HIS MONEY
DOESN'T WANT THE RESPONSIBILITY
DOESN'T UNDERSTAND THE RUSH
AND CAN'T MAKE UP HIS MIND.

THE PINK OR REDDER COLOUR OF
FLAMINGOS COMES FROM
**CAROTENOID**
**PROTEINS**
IN THEIR DIET

DON'T
**STOP**
**VIVA**
**PERIOD**

**MUSCLE**
**SPASMS**
IN THE EYELID

3.8

## Referencing

It is extremely good practice to reference details of every source you use during the course of your research, in order to create a record that you can refer back to. You may need to speak to an interviewee more than once, for example, or you might want to refer back to texts or Internet articles for more detail, or simply need to present sources to your client. Accurate referencing is essential for all of these things. It can also identify further avenues that you can explore.

There are many ways to reference your sources, and the most familiar, such as the Harvard referencing system, are associated with academic work. Whichever method you choose, it is important to stick to it throughout your project, so that everything is referenced consistently. Your research will generate lists of resources such as books, magazines and websites – if details of these are listed clearly in one place, it will help you return to important information at a later date with very little searching.

You may want to use quotations within your findings to prove the validity of your decisions, and it is vital that these are correctly attributed; this information should include the name of the author and source as well as where the work was accessed; whether it is from a book, film or website.

Detailed referencing gives you the chance to build up a list of key texts which will be a valuable resource you can refer back to when working on future projects. This list should be built on consistently as you progress as a designer.

## Harvard referencing system

Harvard University developed its own system for referencing academic sources, which is now widely used. When referencing a book, the following details are required:

- Author name
- Year of publication
- Title
- City of publication
- Publisher

You may also include details of the chapter, and the page number for a specific quote.

The result is that you can quickly locate what you are looking for with just a glance at the reference.

3.9
**Advanced Search, 2011**
*Morey Talmor*

This project references the digital world that we all experience daily; the social networks, blogs, emails and personal computer interfaces that have created a new culture. Morey's project looks at this new culture from a faux-anthropological perspective, presenting the study in the form of a cultural atlas using symbols and images from the digital world.

**3.9**

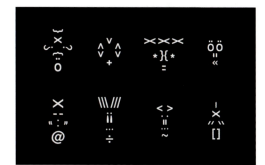

**There are many ways that you can record and document your research findings, but these should be consistent and appropriate to the context of your work. It is worth spending some time in the planning stages of your project considering which methods may work best for you.**

The best tools should be accessible, easy to manage and suitable for the task. It is useful to familiarize yourself with the options that are available to help you record and document your research. You may need to capture information as diverse as a particular environment, a person's reaction, or a textual reference – this will be done more effectively if you've already made decisions about what should be recorded, how and why.

## Physical resources

During any project, it is wise to keep tools at hand to record your ideas and findings as they happen, as insights can come at awkward times. You may struggle with an idea for days, only for the solution to come to you just as you are getting into bed – having a pen and paper to hand ensures inspiration and ideas are not lost.

A sketchbook is often the best way of compiling insights, research and resources, as well as keeping them in order. Carrying one or more sketchbooks will help document a range of findings if coupled with the right materials. A pen or pencil will suffice for notes and drawings, but a charcoal pencil allows rubbings of objects to be made, and coloured markers will help draw out explanatory charts and diagrams.

When interviewing, the most obvious way of recording answers may be to gather paperwork, but it can be more useful to record the answers with a Dictaphone, as people generally respond in a less formal way when speaking. You could also video the interviews, as this will allow you to read more into the way a person reacts physically to a new product or design, or engages with a website.

**3.10—3.12**
**OPO.MIX**
*Atelier Nunes e Pã*

This book is a record of an event called 'Espírito do Douro' which took place in the Oporto and Rio Douro area of Portugal. The book was given to all the parties involved by the Sonae group (one of Portugal's largest companies) as a memento. The book juxtaposes images of old and new, creating a dynamic dialogue between the images.

3.10

3.11

3.12

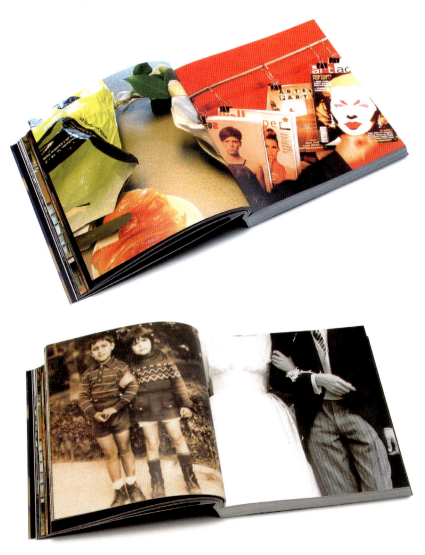

As photographs give people an imaginary possession of a past that is unreal, they also help people to take possession of space in which they are insecure.

Susan Sontag

### 3.13—3.14
### Nostalgia & Berlin
### *Ally Carter* (a student at the University of Brighton, UK)

Experimental exploration of nostalgia and memory, using the medium of a traditional exercise book. To create this, collated prints and archival imagery was printed onto a book that had been taken apart, and was then reconstructed. This method allowed an element of chance to impart on the final work. This work blurs the boundary between traditional design and illustration, as Ally explains. 'I think it's a good thing that ideas of what exactly constitutes design or illustration are rapidly shifting. However you specifically define this crossover – be it through the recent trends in the crafting of photographic collages, or certain processes of abstraction that allow for happy accidents to occur – the creation of imagery for the purposes of communication is a language common to both illustrator and designer.'

3.13

3.14

3.15

## Online resources

Blogs are a flexible digital alternative to a physical sketchbook. Keeping an up-to-date blog allows you to save and cross-reference research materials by adding meta tags. A good blog can also act as a promotional tool, demonstrating that its creator is informed, active and interested. Many people are offered jobs as a result of their blogs, simply because the employer can see they know what they are talking about.

An archive of images is one of the most useful tools any designer can possess and there are many online resources that will assist you in managing one. When starting a project it is a good idea to gather as many images of similar and complementary items as possible. If the brief is to design a new perfume bottle, for example, it will not be possible to view every competitor on the market, but a simple online search will allow you to build up a pictorial archive.

To complement this, it is also useful to create a bank of inspirational imagery that might jump-start the creative process. By continually collecting, you will ensure that you have a thorough visual resource. However, you must be careful how this is used and ensure that a reference is kept of where the images were sourced from – images found on the Internet are protected by copyright in the same way books and texts are, so it is prudent to gain permission before anything is used or even referenced.

**3.15—3.17**
**coffeemademedoit.com – blog**
*Simon Ålander*

With the use of new technology, blogs are now easily accessible, allowing almost anyone to set one up and almost anyone to view it. Blogs allow designers to showcase their work in a colloquial format, instead of creating portfolio pages on websites. They also enable designers to update their work regularly, keeping people interested and creating a fan base of 'followers'.

Simon Ålander's coffeemademedoit.com blog allows him to share his work in an informal way, but each project on his blog is also linked to the full version on his website. The beauty of a blog is that it allows you to show experiments (See figures 3.16 and 3.17) as well as final resolved work.

3.16

3.17

## Studio interview:

### Brian Rea

Brian Rea is a designer, artist and illustrator working in Los Angeles, USA. His unique style is a blend of design and craft, and often involves the repetition of words, epigrams and lists.

**What does research mean to you?**

Getting my head around a topic is super helpful as a foundation, but having something to say about the topic I am researching is equally important.

**Where do you start with a brief?**

I make lists, lots of them. Sometimes the words stay as words and sometimes these develop into drawings.

**What methods of research do you find to be most effective?**

Photography, travel, Google and being a really good listener.

**Where do you find inspiration?**

I shoot a lot of photos – sometimes these make their way into pieces. Also places and people I grew up around; unusual things I see each day; elderly people; patterns; odd, laughable, sad, sweet, still moments...I love it when the remarkably simple is amazing.

3.18

**3.18**
**Lists**

One of many visual and text based lists that Brian creates as part of his research and development process. Here, various fishing flies produce a whimsical illustration.

**3.19**
**Osama Portrait**

This illustration of Osama bin Laden for *New York* magazine, art directed by Chris Dixon, creates a haunting image through the use of negative space.

3.19

Determining who will be the end-user of your designs is a key part of the research process. In this task, you will identify a member of your audience and build a profile of them. The following visualizing tool is used by many design companies to help consider the right approach and direction (methodology) for their research, and then consider how this can be employed to help develop their designs (aims).

**Brief**

Look through magazine advertisements from a weekend supplement, and pick a single luxury product. From here, try to determine the following by making assumptions about the marketplace of the goods:

- Is the product aimed mainly at men or women?

- What would the rough income of the intended audience be?

- Would the intended audience have a family, be married, or be single?

- Would they have a lot of spending power?

- Is it likely the intended audience would own their home?

From here you may like to build a fuller picture of this fictional audience member by considering:

- What would their weekly food shop consist of?

- Which clothing brands might they buy?

- What car might they drive?

**Project objectives**

- To better judge the audience for an intended brief.

- To create a detailed profile of a fictional audience member.

**Recommended reading related to this project**

Graves, P (2010). *Consumerology: The Market Research Myth, the Truth about Consumer Behaviour and the Psychology of Shopping.* Nicholas Brealey Publishing

Hall, S (ed) (1997). *Representation. Cultural Representations and Signifying Practices*. Sage Publications

Klein, N (2010). *No Logo.* Fourth Estate

Raymond, M (2010). *The Trend Forecaster's Handbook*. Laurence King Publishing

Roberts, L (2006). *Good: An Introduction to Ethics in Graphic Design*. AVA Publishing

Sharp, B (2010). *How Brands Grow: What Marketers Don't Know*. Oxford University Press

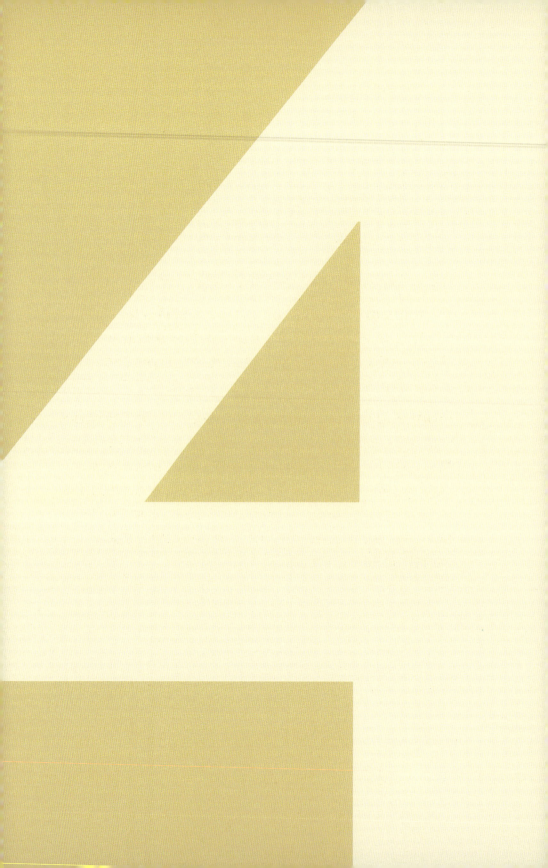

## Chapter 4 – Conducting research

**This chapter focuses on practical research techniques, how you can apply each of them and at what points in your project they are likely to be most relevant.**

From audience and market research, to fieldwork and process-based methods, we look at how different techniques can be used to engage with your audience, help generate ideas and inform the development of your work, from your initial concept all the way to the final material and construction choices.

**Thorough and precise audience research is key to a successful project, and to achieve this you will need to carefully select the people you speak to. Looking into demographics and selecting the best representatives is vital – you should remain <u>reflexive/ reflective</u> throughout the process.**

Audience research can be undertaken in a number of ways, from one-to-one interviews to focus groups and audience tests. Choosing the right method is important, and will depend on which stage of the research process you are at. Tests can only take place once there is something to trial, but consumer opinions can be judged from the earliest stage, by discussing your ideas.

Strong audience research will also help you gain the trust of your client. They are likely to be more positive about your progress and designs if you can place them alongside provable results.

This section introduces some of the many methods that will provide the framework for successful audience research and lead to creative and targeted outcomes.

**Reflexive**
Reflexivity refers to the relationship between cause and effect; with each affecting the other. You must constantly reflect on how your findings are influencing your research, and adjust as necessary.

**Reflective**
Being reflective is the art of looking back at your work and considering what has gone well, what could be improved upon, and what you can learn from this experience that can be applied to future projects.

**Approaching audience members**

Your audience know what they want from your product and they are often willing to share this information. But how should you contact them?

Your client may have a bank of contacts for you to approach. If they do not, there are numerous other options. The most straightforward method is to simply speak to people in the street (though caution should be exercised when taking this direct approach). There are also marketing and research agencies that specialize in user testing and focus groups – these will have a host of relevant contacts. An online search will identify relevant research agencies.

Social media has made it very easy to identify and contact people with particular interests. Questions can be asked over long distances, allowing many contacts to be reached that may previously have been inaccessible.

## Participant and non-participant observation

Often used in sociology, participant and non-participant observation techniques can be used to gain an insight into human behaviour and, crucially in the case of designers, the behaviour of consumers.

In participant observation, the audience is aware that their reactions are being monitored because an interviewer will be present. In non-participant observation, they may not be aware, as they may be observed from a distance or questioned by a third party.

Covert non-participant observation may be as simple as observing members of the public to see how they react to certain stimuli. For example, if they try a new flavour of ice-cream, do they seem to enjoy it? An interviewer may not announce themselves, they may simply engage in conversation with the participant. In this case, there are ethical issues to consider – is it fair to use research you have gathered from subjects who did not know they were part of a research project?

Participant observation usually takes the form of observation followed by questioning. It can be conducted one-to-one, or in a focus group. It is the best way to create a relationship with your audience – the more familiar you are with them, the more likely you will gain positive and truthful results. However familiar you become to your interviewees, it is likely that you'll be viewed with some suspicion as your agenda is to question them and inform a third party of the results. When working this way, you also run the risk of participants giving you the answers they think you want to hear.

## Questionnaires

A questionnaire is a form designed to gather statistical information about a specific group of people, with data most often gathered through face-to-face interaction with the interviewee. Typically, questions will be targeted at the chosen group in order to gain opinions and information about a given issue, and the interviewees should be chosen for their ability to offer a particular insight. If you are designing for a specific demographic, these are the people you should first question.

The form may contain questions that yield both qualitative and quantitative results (see page 28). Questions designed to gain easily quantifiable answers will be 'closed'. These may include asking the interviewee for:

• Factual information such as their age, gender, occupation.

• Attitudes on particular issues, such as government policies.

• Preferences on media, politics or fashion.

• Behavioural trends, such as monthly expenditure on specific items or visits to certain destinations.

The answers to these questions will help you identify trends and patterns that should indicate a direction for your designs. You may also ask more 'open' questions to gain a qualitative response. In this case, you need to allow space and time for the interviewee to describe their understanding of the subject. This is often of most use when you are starting a project and want to gain an understanding of the context, and also when you are near the end of a project and want to monitor its effectiveness.

**4.1**
**Bloody Good Wine**
*Cameron Sandage/Chase Farthing*
**(students at Portland State University, USA)**

Having a clear understanding of a target market will make research and design development more effective. In this project, provocative naming and typography is selected to reach a previously untapped market.

'The inspiration behind the bottles was to promote wine consumption with our target market of 21–28-year-old college males. We wanted to create a bottle that would be familiar to men that are generally beer drinkers. In order to do this we decided that we could use a screw-top style dark glass bottle with a mini cork to mimic how a true wine bottle is constructed.'

Primary research and field study through questionnaires and surveys revealed that this demographic found drinking wine to be 'un-masculine', and this led to the selection of a more masculine 'beer' bottle.

4.1

## Surveys

A survey is in many ways similar to a questionnaire, but it tends to focus more on gathering facts in an anonymous way and less on opinions and taste. Surveys tend to be employed to monitor numbers, such as the size of a particular population. This information is often broken down into sub-categories, such as age, income and dependants.

Surveys are often employed within retail graphics to monitor competitors and market share. This can include looking at elements such as the numbers of products and sales of rival brands. Results from this can be developed into aims that the client may use to monitor the effectiveness of your designs. An eye-catching campaign will be expected to increase the footfall near your client's products and, as an extension of this, their sales.

A survey can be conducted in person or it can be a remote task. With new technologies, a traditional phone or mail survey can now be conducted online through social media sites or emailed to a virtually limitless number of people.

The advantage of a survey over a traditional face-to-face questionnaire is that the format – mail, phone, or email – is considerably more cost-effective and allows you to reach a far wider demographic. One downside is that it lacks the human interaction gained when conducting a questionnaire, so it is hard to build up a rapport with the interviewee.

A telephone survey says that 51 per cent of college students drink until they pass out at least once a month. The other 49 per cent didn't answer the phone.

Craig Kilborn

### The survey process

The survey process has several distinct stages:

- Defining the demographic or group you are sampling.
- Setting a framework of what you want to measure.
- Specifying a method.
- Determining the sample size.
- Implementing the plan.
- Collecting the data.

Some of the ways in which an audience group, or sample, can be selected for a survey are described below.

### Probability sampling

Probability sampling involves a random selection of participants – everyone has an equal chance of being selected, and no groups are intentionally excluded.

### Non-probability sampling

In non-probability sampling certain groups or clusters are excluded. For example, men or women over the age of 40.

### Convenience sampling

Sometimes called 'grab' or 'accidental' sampling, this is a method of convenience, sampling the groups that you have immediate access to.

4.2

**4.2**
**'I'm Eating a Banana'**
*Brian Rea*
*Antenna* **magazine**
**Art director: Shanna Greenberg**

A satirical take on the current preoccupation
with social networking and connectivity.

## Interviews

An interview is a great way to gather in-depth responses to a particular problem. One of the benefits of an interview over a questionnaire or survey is that they are usually conducted with a small group of people or an individual, and allow you to deviate from the original questions should an interesting or unexpected line of enquiry occur.

Another benefit of a person-to-person interview is that the candidate is more likely to give honest and positive responses, as they are more engaged in the process. When a person is asked to tick boxes in a questionnaire or survey, they can become bored and vary their answers just to show that they are paying attention, so their response may not be entirely truthful. When you sit with an interviewee, you will find it easier to stay on track and gain a far deeper understanding of the subject.

If it is not possible to meet an interviewee, you can use webchats or telephone conversations. These can be more difficult to manage than a face-to-face meeting, so it is essential that you come across as trustworthy and personable if you use this method.

Interviews can be structured, semi-structured, or unstructured, depending on the type of response you want to elicit. If the conversation is less rigid, it is easier to be more personable, but you may find it more difficult to focus and get the information you need. If the interview is structured, it is important that you come across as human and easy-going – even if you receive information counter to your expectations – as you do not want the interviewee to feel as if they are being interrogated.

### Interview tips

- Research the subject well, and know what you are asking for.
- Have clear aims and objectives.
- Write a list of questions or talking points, but allow yourself to move away from these if necessary.
- Be calm, objective, professional and approachable.
- Offer your interviewee refreshments and a comfortable environment.
- Record the interview – transcripts are also useful.
- Make sure you get the answers you need without being confrontational.
- Always follow up the interview with a thank-you email.

# There is no substitute for face-to-face reporting and research.

Thomas Friedman

4.3

**4.3**
**UK Fashion Hub**
*Gavin Ambrose*

The UK Fashion Hub is a proposal for the future legacy of the Press and Broadcast Centres at the Queen Elizabeth Olympic Park, Stratford, London. They have developed four essential principles to cover all areas of their target market: education, manufacturing, events and commerce.

The UK Fashion Hub conducted and filmed a series of unstructured interviews with a variety of professionals, including clothing manufacturers, apprentices, business directors and regeneration experts to gauge views, thoughts and opinions on their proposal.

## Focus groups

Focus groups are a good way of conducting a concentrated audience test that provides reliable qualitative data. This method seeks answers from multiple people over a short, concentrated period and relies heavily on the interactions and conversations within the group.

With a group of carefully selected members of the target audience in a room, you can quickly and effectively determine the usefulness and appropriateness of your idea or concept. This method allows the subjects to interact with one another and discuss ideas in a way that may help you develop your work further.

It is vital to ensure that your focus group contains a representative cross-section of your audience, otherwise you may not cover everyone's needs equally. You should also make sure that an open discussion takes place and that everyone is heard equally – a dominant personality can influence others in the group and affect the discussion.

A focus group can be either formal or informal, but it is important that the subjects feel at ease so they are willing to give honest answers. A useful number of people to speak to at once is between four and ten – if the group is too large it is likely some members will be left out and might not be heard. When the focus group is in session, a moderator should ensure that the discussion stays on track and that everyone gets a chance to speak. You should also ensure that the space is comfortable and free from distractions.

All focus group meetings should be recorded and a full transcript generated, to ensure that you can accurately represent the opinions of the participants.

### Focus group tips

Ask your focus group candidates for their opinions and feedback regarding every aspect of your design work, including:

- Aesthetics – the overall look of the design work, whether it appeals and if it could be improved.

- Functionality – how easy is it to access and use, and can they suggest better or more pleasing ways it could be operated?

- Price – question how much they would pay for the final piece, and what they would consider good value for money.

- Placement – discuss the context the work will be seen in, so that you can assess how noticeable it will be in terms of its surroundings.

- Competition – how does it compare to other, similar products?

## Case studies

Case studies that have been created by dedicated researchers can be accessed to help you gain a deep understanding of a particular audience group. These can equally offer an insight into a given subject, event, period of time or organization.

Case studies often contain qualitative (interviews, observations) and quantitative (test results, analysis, statistics) data. The benefit of accessing a case study is that the information within it will often have been gathered over a long period of time – it is likely that much of your own primary research will consist of contemporary information, so these studies can offer a much greater overview that complements your work.

You will often find in these case studies examples of key cases that exemplify good practice, as well as detailed information about how the outcome was achieved. Also you will often find examples of projects that have been implemented – this is particularly useful in helping you to assess whether your outcomes will succeed.

A case study will often be presented to you, but generating your own that showcases successful research and outcomes is a good way of presenting your work in a concise, designed and organized way. This is especially useful when presenting final work in a portfolio or on your website – a short text that describes the process and success of a project will give it context and give a client confidence when looking to hire you.

**To understand how the market is perceived, retail, advertising and marketing companies have developed strategies to help them predict whether a product or service will be successful.**

When a company identifies the need for a new product or aims to enhance the profile of an existing one, they will undertake market research to measure and analyse the ways goods are disseminated from the producer to the consumer. This process looks at what makes a product desirable, as well as looking at the broad market and competing brands.

4.4

### Conducting market research

Market research is as relevant to an individual designer as it is to a large company. To find out what already exists in the area you are designing for, you can research products and services by scouring the Internet, visiting outlets where the items are sold, or by looking through the websites of the manufacturers. It is also worth trying to track down the companies that designed the items you find, as this may demonstrate what other companies are trying to achieve.

Market research can also be conducted from a consumer's point of view, and this can uncover insightful and unfiltered opinions. Many shopping websites allow consumers to

4.5

review the products they buy and these reviews often highlight areas that you could improve upon, such as ease of use, design and durability. These reviews will also give you an insight into what people like about particular products, which will help you understand the motives behind a purchase.

To make the most of market research, you will need to collate the findings of your audience research and anything else you've discovered that is pertinent to your project. You can use this to form the basis of a report against which you can test the feasibility of your proposal. To ensure you have the right information available, it is useful to imagine this stage at the beginning of the research cycle and consider what you will need.

This is often one of the most creative parts of the research cycle as you may have to respond to minute detail, or look for ways to enhance the perception of a brand. To do this effectively you need to consider the values of the audience and the perceived values of the brand – a mismatch of these two elements will result in consumers being uninterested or even against the product or service being offered. If a consumer can align themselves with your product, it is more likely that they will buy into it.

**4.4—4.6**
**Habit, 2010**
*Morey Talmor*

This packaging design was created for Habit, a company that specializes in drug rehabilitation and cessation products. Each product is packaged in a simple black bottle or container, with the aim of providing a discreet experience to those undergoing rehabilitation.

4.6

107

## Marketing strategies

A marketing strategy is a plan that aims to deliver measurable results related to the growth of a company or product. To achieve this, market research will map out competitors and rivals, and key attributes that the product needs in order to grow. Commonly, it will look first at market leaders that present a challenge in terms of profit and recognition, but will also consider what niche companies exist. Analysing their success will reveal information that can point towards potential areas of growth or improvement; this process is often recorded through a SWOT analysis.

A marketing strategy is designed to reduce risk and ensure success, but it is not an exact science and factors such as the state of the economy or changing trends also act as variables. It is likely the company will have conducted a large amount of research into whether there is a need for their new product before commissioning a designer, and this will shape the goals and limitations of the brief they issue.

## SWOT analysis

This is a process by which you compare your product or idea to the market and carefully map its:

- Strengths – what you are currently doing well.

- Weaknesses – where you need to improve.

- Opportunities – areas in which you could achieve.

- Threats – areas in which you are unlikely to do better than your competitors.

The results from a SWOT analysis can be turned into a strategic plan with points of action which can be measured, tested and refined through the course of your project.

If a weakness, such as the consumer not being aware of a product, is identified, market research can be carried out to determine the best way to reach the audience in order to address this.

**4.7**
**A SWOT diagram**

A SWOT diagram is used to plot how a product or service is perceived. Generally speaking, your strengths and opportunities are viewed as positive, while your weaknesses and threats are classed as negative. It is worth noting that your strengths and weaknesses are internal factors – you control these – while the opportunities and threats are external forces, that you can't necessarily control in the same way.

Within each of these four sections, the detail will vary depending on the type of brand or product. Shown are some general themes to consider.

4.7

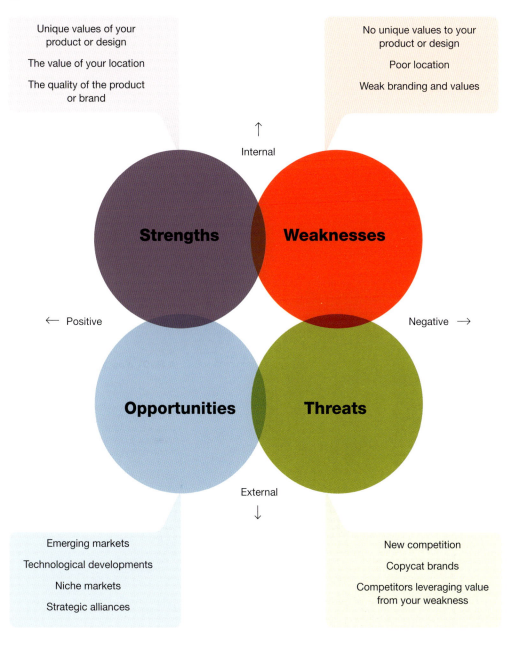

Unique values of your
product or design

The value of your location

The quality of the product
or brand

No unique values to your
product or design

Poor location

Weak branding and values

↑
Internal

**Strengths**

**Weaknesses**

← Positive

Negative →

**Opportunities**

**Threats**

External
↓

Emerging markets

Technological developments

Niche markets

Strategic alliances

New competition

Copycat brands

Competitors leveraging value
from your weakness

## Advertising strategy

An advertising strategy is a plan for the way a product or service will be presented to the world. This is best implemented once you really understand your audience, as their needs and wants will have to be clearly addressed. An assessment of the product will be made and a strategy and action plan will be devised and presented to the client.

Research into developing an advertising strategy will look at how the company and product are perceived and how they sit alongside their competitors in the marketplace, then a brief will be formed that either:

- Looks to attract new customers.

- Attracts customers that would usually buy a rival brand.

- Modifies the image of the company and enhances its presence or personality.

To achieve this, a target consumer is identified, and their behaviour defined in terms of how they interact with the product and which similar brands they use. By using targeted questionnaires, interviews and thorough observation, this is extended to give a clear picture of how they live as a consumer.

A consumer's needs and desires are always played out through their purchases, so it's vital that any designer has a good idea of who their target buyer is and what they want their purchases to say about them. This understanding leads to the development of a strategy that can be presented to the client, detailing the message the company should aim to promote and the ways in which it can be communicated.

**4.8**
**Ecko Unltd.**
*Fuse Collective*

This Ecko Unltd. advertisement by Fuse Collective is a fusion of elements of youth culture, street style, video games and illustration. Ecko is a brand that embraces emerging trends and graphic styles. This design encompasses their values; skate culture, action sports, and art. These values are what make the brand, and the visual expression of this is articulated into an intriguing new reality.

Advertising people who ignore research are as dangerous as generals who ignore decodes of enemy signals.

David Ogilvy

There are many research methods and tools that can be employed from the comfort of the studio, but often the best way to discover new things is to get out and look at how people live. Face-to-face contact will always be the best way to get an honest response from a person.

Consumers are often willing to share their opinions, but they will not come to you – it is your job to seek them out.

In this section we take a look at some of the specifically field-based research methods that can be employed to gain a deeper understanding of audience, context and trends, as well as helping with problem solving.

## Fieldwork

Fieldwork is research conducted in the environment where your work will eventually exist. This is an active part of research and it will help identify resources, audience and existing work. The benefit of this form of research is that it allows you to see firsthand how products and services are selected and interacted with by consumers. This observation can help identify audience members and develop ideas for style, message, materials and processes.

Fieldwork can be a large undertaking, however. Within a design company, it is likely that a group of designers will conduct this part of the research together. Working with others will yield greater results as, quite simply, more people can cover more ground. It is also useful to work with others when analysing your results – a well documented study will normally result in a bank of photographs, notes, audio/video recordings and, most importantly, leads that can be followed up with questionnaires and surveys.

Fieldwork should be analysed and reflected upon carefully. When looking at the results, you should refer back to your brief and ask, 'Is this knowledge that will aid the progression of my project?'

4.9

**4.9—4.11**
**Hard Times, the Big Issue Twentieth Anniversary Exhibition**
*Paul Wenham-Clarke/Neil Leonard*

*The Big Issue* magazine is sold by homeless and vulnerably-housed people in the UK, and was set up with the intention of helping its vendors to earn a legitimate income and rebuild their lives. In 2011, it celebrated its twentieth anniversary by commissioning award-winning photographer Paul Wenham-Clarke to undertake a project entitled Hard Times. Paul interviewed and photographed some of the many people that have been helped by this remarkable charity and the resulting photographs toured the UK as an exhibition and were compiled in this volume.

**4.10**

**4.11**

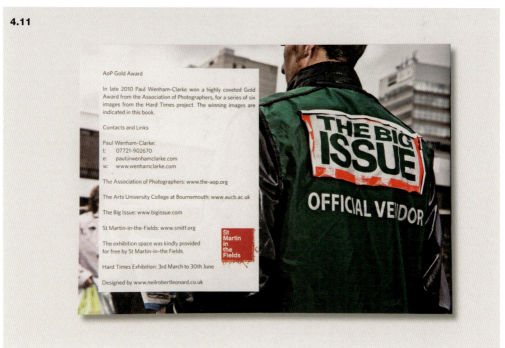

**4.12**

**4.12—4.13**
**Hannah Turner Ceramics**
*Andrew Hussey*

Graphic designer Andrew Hussey worked with Hannah Turner, an illustrator and ceramicist, to develop a visual language and appropriate tone of voice, utilizing the 'chirpy' nature of Hannah's illustration style. Their main aim was to create an appropriate identity, marketing materials and email campaign for Hannah's ceramic products.

Andrew explains the importance of fieldwork in this: 'I have really immersed myself in Hannah's world as much as possible. I often visit her studio and photograph her creative environment. So much of her work is about her as an individual, her personality and her environment. I have the ongoing challenge of getting a balance between the commercial aspect of what she does – competing with the Cath Kidstons of that world – and appropriately reflecting her as an individual.'

The appeal of 1950s cartoons is evident in my designs. I love their vintage illustrative style – playful, yet drawing reference from a very modern cultural aesthetic.

Hannah Turner

4.13

4.14

## Trendspotting

Trendspotting is a form of field-based research that aims to identify trends that are about to emerge. It is primarily used within the fashion industry, but can also be valuable within areas of product and graphic design.

Trendspotting is conducted at street level. A trendspotter will observe and talk to people who are deemed to have an interesting or innovative personal style. These people are usually not designers or celebrities, but ordinary people. Once this person or group is identified, they are quizzed about the origins and influences of their style. After several people have been interviewed a report is generated that indicates elements a company should consider when developing cutting-edge products or services.

The information gathered relates to personal style, but by looking at trends such as pattern, colour and material, the results can easily be applied to graphic design, as all areas of art and design feed into and inform one another.

## Coolhunting

Another method of field-based research used to find out about 'the next big thing' is coolhunting. Companies employ coolhunters to investigate emerging trends and styles in youth culture, aiming to determine what is currently considered as 'cool'. This may range from fashion, media, and technology, to popular culture as a whole.

This form of research is covert in its information gathering techniques, as many young people would find the targeted questioning of a corporate market research agency off-putting. As a result, much of it is conducted without the full knowledge of the participants.

The reports created by coolhunters will form a base of research that can be developed into concepts and ideas. However, identified trends are often not fully taken on due to the individual and occasionally obscure nature of their beginnings – something too ambiguous will not have the mass appeal many designers and clients seek.

**4.14**
**The Hanging Man**
*Banksy*

Don't be afraid to show and trial your work and research. Political graffiti artists, such as Banksy, revel in the public exhibition of their work. It could be argued that ideas don't live in sketchbooks, and that they die there. Research, develop and show your work. Trends emerge from unlikely sources. As a practising designer you should be aware of movements within graphic design, but also in art, music and film.

## Crowdsourcing

Crowdsourcing is a method of field-based research often employed to solve problems. A select crowd is issued with tasks or asked to consider an issue, then asked for potential solutions. Once responses are gathered, the crowd is asked to vote for the best solution.

The crowd can be sourced from those already interested in the subject and willing to give their time, or from online communities. One of the benefits of this is that both of these groups are likely to offer their services for free, so the research costs are kept low. Ethically, this can be an issue – if a company makes large amounts of money through a product that has been crowdsourced, it is often hard to track who is responsible for the concept and offer them appropriate credit or financial rewards. However, by working in this way, you can access a large workforce; this means that problems can be solved more quickly than with questionnaires or focus groups alone.

Changes in technology have seen crowdsourcing used most effectively on the web. The ability to connect with thousands of users via social networks has meant that groups can easily be assembled to work together. This allows individuals to assemble teams with little or no financial backing, instead offering credit or finished goods in return for support. However, the open source nature of the web means that many people are willing to offer their time and ideas just because the subject is of interest – rewards are often not expected.

### Crowdsourcing

'Crowdsourcing' is a portmanteau word, made from 'crowd' and 'outsourcing'. Jeff Howe first used the term in a June 2006 *Wired* magazine article 'The Rise of Crowdsourcing', and it has since been adopted as a working method for many businesses, particularly when using new technologies. This community-based problem solving relies on mass collaboration to find solutions. The beauty of crowdsourcing is that the person most able to solve the problem will.

Crowdsourcing is the process by which the power of the many can be leveraged to accomplish feats that were once the province of a specialized few.

Jeff Howe

4.15

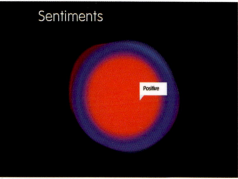

**4.15**
**A Christmas Tweet**
*Studio Output*

Tapping into social media and crowdsourcing, Studio Output created an application to monitor festive themes mentioned on Twitter – music, sentiments, brands, gifts and family vs money. Each theme was represented visually on the site, and increased or decreased in size according to how much it was being tweeted about.

The site worked by querying tweets which contained the word 'Christmas' and key words related to the five themes above. After more than two million tweets had been recorded, the data was analysed, producing some startling results. Gemma Ballinger of Studio Output explains, 'We discovered Apple products made up 42 per cent of people's gift lists and that Justin Bieber got more mentions than Jesus!'.

**In addition to audience, market and ideas-based research, it is important that you research and understand the implications of different material or construction choices.**

In many ways these decisions are as important as the design itself. The right processes can add value to a project, and the wrong choices can cause problems with production, durability and presentation. Your audience will read as much into the finish of your work as they will the idea, as this is part of what they are buying into. Again, an understanding of the values and personality of your audience will help you make well-informed design choices.

## Materials, production and construction

When researching the work of other designers, it is important to ask yourself how it has been made. This will give an insight into how you can take your own designs further. When you create new or experimental work, this sort of analysis is crucial. The choice of materials can determine whether a project succeeds or fails.

It is also important to research the cost and sources of the materials you plan to use. If your choice is rare or expensive it will push up the cost of production and increase the price for the client and end-user. You should also consider whether the materials will be fit for purpose. When creating work, a certain lifespan and durability will be expected – does your choice of materials offer this? If not, could it be improved?

As early in your project as possible, you should consider how your work will be produced, as this can have significant cost and time implications. Many designers leave such considerations until after the work is designed. This is a mistake, as knowledge of how your work will be made can affect your designs in a positive and unexpected way. The use of a certain material or construction technique will change how your work is perceived by the audience, and this can also affect its value and prestige.

4.16
Rawganical
*Casper Holden/Randi Sjælland Jensen/Ingeborg Lund (students at the School of Visual Communication, Denmark)*

This experimental packaging uses natural materials, printing stocks and binding ties. The wooden top is a response to basic fieldwork. 'We asked how people treat shampoo bottles to get everything out of the container, and found out that almost everyone puts it upside-down when it's nearly empty.' This led to the development of the sturdy wooden top, which allows the bottle to stand upside-down. 'We researched materials and drew inspiration from the raw materials in the product.'

FACE AND
BODY LOTION

# RAWGANICAL

Instantly balances skin perfectly after
bath or shaving. Silk protein makes skin
firm and smooth, seaweed and witch
hazel provide vitamins and antioxidants.

# Studio interview:

## Jane Trustram

Jane Trustram studied BA (Hons) Graphic Design at University College Falmouth, before completing an MA in Graphic Design at London College of Communication. She has since worked on projects from packaging to editorial, for both British and overseas clients.

## What does research mean to you?

Research is one of the best parts of being a graphic designer! As someone who is hungry for knowledge, I relish the idea of being able to understand a new topic enough to be able to re-represent it in a graphic context.

I like Simon Esterton's three rules of editorial design:

1. Read the copy.
2. Read the copy.
3. Read the copy.

As graphic designers, we deal with other people's content. In order to be able to relay it in an effective way it is important that we understand it fully ourselves first, otherwise we run the risk of misrepresenting it and misleading the audience.

## Where do you start with a brief?

With my eyes and ears. It's important to listen, understand and absorb what the client wants from the brief. If you choose to question this at a later stage, fine, but if you don't fully understand the brief and how the client feels about it and what they want, you will end up wasting a lot of time.

## What methods of research do you find to be most effective?

I think I work quite intuitively. I try to get a feel for a project before I go producing output. It's important to me that I completely understand it, so I will read around my client and their competitors before I start coming up with design solutions.

## Where do you find inspiration?

Everywhere! I rarely switch off and am naturally inquisitive. I find I make connections between day-to-day life and projects without even realizing it. I can get inspiration from walking down the street, sitting in the park, eating, or jogging. I try not to look to other design work for inspiration as I find it clouds your mind, or narrows your scope. Instead, my inspiration comes from outside of the design realm.

**4.17**
**Deconstructing Graphic Design**

This research-based project, undertaken as part of Jane's MA, looked into deconstruction theory and graphic design. She explains, 'Using content and form as my subjects, I performed a deconstruction within the field of graphic design. This left me thinking about form as content, about perception, about imagination and the role of the designer in creating that experience.'

4.17

## Product and customer

Observing people as they shop can give clear indications of the way they make buying choices. Do they go straight for one product, do they browse, or do they ask for advice? This exercise will help you to develop your observational skills in a retail environment.

### Brief

For this exercise, you need to go into a shop and watch people as they purchase one of the following products:

- Electrical goods (television, DVD player, etc.)

- Health and beauty products (cosmetics or health products)

You should pick one particular product and make this your focus. From here you can analyse:

- What other products exist in this field?

- How are competitors exhibiting their products?

- The material construction and design choices.

When you see someone buy the product, you can observe what they are wearing and what else they are buying – this can give you some insight into the customer profile.

You may also wish to survey these customers, asking what has attracted them to the particular item, or whether they have bought the product before.

## Project objectives

- Developing primary research skills that can be applied to any product or service.

## Recommended reading related to this project

Arden, P (2003). *It's Not How Good You Are, It's How Good You Want To Be.* Phaidon Press

Barnard, M (2001). *Approaches to Understanding Visual Culture*. Palgrave

Lupton, E and Cole Phillips, J (2008). *Graphic Design: The New Basics*. Princeton Architectural Press

Millman, D (2008). *The Essential Principles of Graphic Design.* Rotovision

Noble, I and Bestley, R (2007). *Visual Research: An Introduction to Research Methodologies in Graphic Design*. AVA Publishing

Pipes, A (2009). *Production for Graphic Designers.* Laurence King Publishing

Poynor, R (2003). *No More Rules: Graphic Design and Postmodernism*. Laurence King Publishing

**Chapter 5 – Using your findings**

**In this chapter we explore how you can interpret, respond to and test your research findings.**

We consider how data can be categorized, synthesized, reflected upon and analysed, and how this can develop and inform your design practice. We also introduce the idea of tests and trials and look at how audience members can assess the effectiveness of your designs and solutions.

This will lead to consideration of further experimentation and development that can be employed to finalize your ideas and solutions.

**Research can be a difficult process if you don't have a clear idea of what you are looking for. The steps you take to guide you from the brief to the outcome of your project should be logical and informed by your findings, so clearly understanding the results of your research is essential.**

There are many ways that research results can be looked at and understood, but it is crucial to take time to reflect on the information you have gathered, analyse your findings and then use the process of synthesis to narrow your focus and draw clear conclusions.

## Categorization

The worst thing that can happen during a project is for important findings to be lost – if you are nearing a solution which is reliant on a key piece of information, you need it to be at hand quickly, so categorizing and organizing your results from the earliest stage is vital. There are many approaches to categorizing your findings, but two terms commonly used are typology and topography.

Typology describes the study of types, or groups, of things. This is often used to gain an overview of existing work within a particular context. For example, if you are designing a logo for a clothing brand, you may compile a typology of existing designs to gain an understanding of what works in this context.

Topography describes the appearance of the work you are studying, and the relationship between the components that make it up, in a detailed and systematic way. Historically, topographies have been used to map places, detailing the surface and shape of the earth, so this can be particularly useful when looking at work in a specific location. However, this process can also be employed to look at specific points within history (the style of a decade), populations (movement, size and growth) and objects (placement, size and material structure).

**Typology**
A typology is the classification and study of general types. The term is commonly used in archaeology and the social sciences, as well as in design.

**Topography**
Topography is a detailed description or mapping of something; whilst this term often refers to physical locations, it can also be used to detail the physical features of an object.

## Synthesis

Every project generates a mass of information, from which you will need to pick out the elements that are of most use, and discard the rest – this is the process of synthesis. Narrowing down your research results in this way will help you focus the direction in which you wish to take your project. Synthesis can apply to any part of the research process – every choice you make through your project will take you through a broad investigative stage, after which you will narrow your focus.

To do this effectively, you must refer back to the brief and determine whether the research is helping you to respond to it. You should consider whether the work is meeting the needs of the audience that you identified – usability tests and focus groups will help here. There are many additional considerations, such as cost, availability and access to relevant technologies, but all of these factors will help you to synthesize your findings and reach a logical solution.

When you are working for a client, you are likely to have limited time and resources, so you will need to concentrate on the most promising research avenues. To determine what these are, you will have to look broadly, but make a decision at each juncture about whether that is the best option to pursue. Strands of research that you discard during synthesis can always be revisited later on, if they are needed.

The goal is to transform data into information, and information into insight.

Carly Fiorina

## Reflection

Reflection is a key tool for any graphic designer – if you do not reflect on what you have done, you will not be able to learn from it and move forwards. Taking time to reflect on your research results is essential in order to understand and properly respond to them. Research is not just a process of amassing facts – the real work is in comparing methods and asking which has given the most valuable information, and whether you have uncovered what you need to succeed.

To determine whether the research activities you've undertaken are the right ones, you can draw comparisons between different processes or studies. Were the answers to your questionnaires roughly in line with information gathered through surveys? If not, you should ask why – you may have asked the wrong questions, or it's possible you have uncovered something new that others have missed.

Asking what your results mean is vital if you are to use research to its full potential. If 80 per cent of a group surveyed say they prefer blue to red, was this because of the options presented, or due to other influences? You may need to dig deep and ask further questions to really understand your results.

When concluding a project, it is also worth reflecting on what went well and what you may do differently in the future. This can be difficult, as it involves looking at your own strengths and weaknesses, but if you are honest it will help you progress your career. Reflecting on success is easy, but identifying where you need to grow is a far more effective tool that will help you to achieve great things.

**5.1**
**T-shirt design for UNIQLO contest**
*Serse Rodriguez*

This T-shirt design was created in response to a contest held by Japanese clothing manufacturer UNIQLO. Serse explains how he applied reflection to this, and to his other projects: 'When I finish a project I usually have a new one waiting, so I prefer to leave the completed project to one side and not come back to it until a few days or weeks have passed. I come back to it to analyse how and why it has turned out the way it has and what has influenced and inspired me. I look at the design drafts, the ideas and all the twists and turns that the project has taken to reach the end result.'

5.1

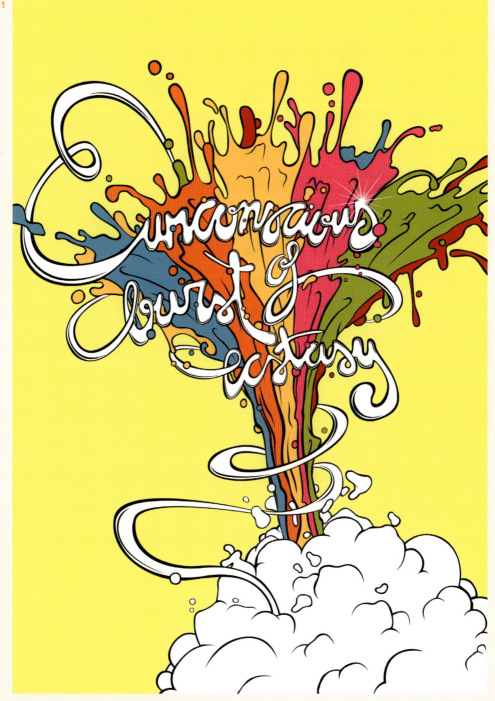

## Content analysis

Content analysis is a method that can be used to analyse research findings. It is particularly effective in interpreting the results of questionnaires and surveys, as it looks at how responses can be grouped together, by identifying common characteristics. By measuring the frequency of certain words, you can look for themes that can be categorized and classified. Because this looks to remove personal opinions and preferences from answers, the data should be reliable and consistent.

First, you should identify the units the content can be broken down into, then clearly define the focus of your study – at this point you need to ensure that you consider all of the possibilities for categorization, as you may have to refine your results at a later point and break the data down further. Breaking data down into manageable categories makes the responses easier to quantify.

This method can also be used to measure the occurrence of visual elements. When researching advertising campaigns, for example, you may wish to determine the frequency of male or female subjects, the number of textual devices or the palette of colours. To do this, you would define a sample, either at random, or by collecting a definitive range pertinent to a specific area. You would then carefully choose the elements you are looking for – you may wish to keep categories broad, such as the colour red, or you may wish to break this down further into hues and tones. From here you would document the frequency of each element and this should suggest a good way forward for your work.

**Harold Lasswell**
Noted for being ahead of his time in employing a variety of methodological approaches, Harold Lasswell (1902–1978), formulated the core questions of content analysis. This is a standard methodology in the social sciences when looking at communication content. The model represents the process of communication.

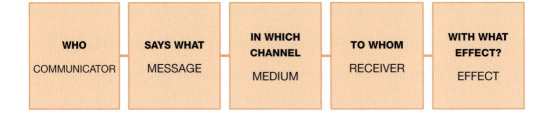

| WHO | SAYS WHAT | IN WHICH CHANNEL | TO WHOM | WITH WHAT EFFECT? |
|---|---|---|---|---|
| COMMUNICATOR | MESSAGE | MEDIUM | RECEIVER | EFFECT |

# Who says what, in which channel, to whom, with what effect?

**Harold Lasswell**

How you respond to the research you gather will determine the path your project takes. As we've seen, synthesis, analysis and reflection help you determine what will be of most use, but your responses to your findings will be influenced by your knowledge of design.

Audience tests may show that the majority of people surveyed would prefer a piece of packaging to be red, but having considered several design factors, you may decide this is the wrong approach. The customer – or test audience, in this case – is not always right. Sometimes you need to defy their expectations in order to amaze them. Your understanding of visual language is vital to this.

Eventually, your responses to research findings will have to be turned into proposals for the best solution to the brief, and presented to your client. Once you have developed a solution, it will need to be tested on the audience – this is the point at which you will discover whether your responses to your research findings were the correct ones.

5.3

**5.2—5.4**
**Harvey Milk Wine**
*Emily Hale*
*Photographed by Raine*
*Manley Robertson*

Produced as part of Emily Hale's studies at the Pratt Institute, this packaging was inspired by the US politician and gay rights campaigner, Harvey Milk. The logo is reflective of Milk's positive outlook – is the glass half empty or half full? It uses quotes from Milk that are appropriate to the product: 'I have tasted freedom. I will not give up that which I have tasted. I have a lot more to drink.'

5.2

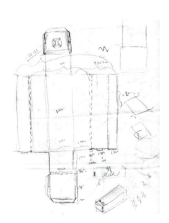

5.4

## Experimentation

Experimentation is the process by which you try things out and ask, 'What if?' Through considered experimentation, you can respond to your research findings and form ideas of how the brief could be solved. These ideas can then be tested against the project's objectives to see if they will lead towards the creation of appropriate solutions.

Experimentation can be open-ended, or strictly controlled, but whichever approach you choose you should continuously relate it to your brief and intended outcome.

Open-ended experimentation allows you to add elements together to see what happens, without a strict rationale. This is something every designer will do as they search for the perfect typeface or colour – trying out the possibilities and observing which combinations work best. Open-ended experimentation can be extremely effective in terms of innovation. It is difficult to think beyond the existing parameters of the brief without a system to help you achieve this, however, so you may want to use lateral thinking exercises to help prompt innovative ideas.

With controlled experimentation, you construct variables around a theme and test them to see which is most effective. This may take the form of material tests, through which you look at durability and strength, or visual tests where you present ideas to an audience to see which ones work best. When employing controlled experimentation as a part of your methodology, careful monitoring is vital. All trials should be recorded in detail, as all results will yield some knowledge that may prove to be useful at later points.

To ensure your work at this stage is leading you in the right direction, you should test your results on potential audience members as you progress.

5.5

**5.5—5.7**
**Experiments in form**
*The Miha Artnak*

These are visual experiments in stretching type in both horizontal and vertical planes. This type of experimental research forms a pattern in Miha's work, of looking, re-looking, thinking and re-thinking. The letters in each example spell the word 'ZEK', a design collective which Miha is part of.

5.6

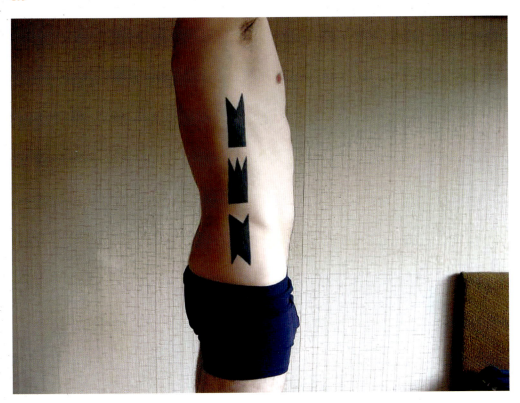

5.7

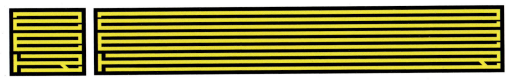

**5.8—5.9**
**Your opinion is irrelevant because I hate you**
*Hannah Richards* (a student at the University of Brighton, UK)

These engaging epigrams and drawings combine to create a work of wit and presence, capturing mundane occurrences of everyday life. 'The combination of text and image has always interested me and I think one can influence the other in a fantastic way. Whereas a lot of graphic design is concerned with how type complements image, the text in my work is more integral – there are two halves to the work and neither is complete without the other. My drawings are purposefully crude and realized quickly, as a way of expressing my ideas very immediately.'

The process of research can take many forms, as Hannah explains: 'I constantly collect objects, read books, watch films and all of that influences me. I need a constant flow of information. For this project I spent a lot of time in the library – there is something more satisfying in photocopying rather then just trawling through the Internet. At the beginning of a project I make a list of ideas, then I go through the list and try to create each image. If it doesn't work, I scrap it; if I like it, I keep it. I don't tend to rely too heavily on other peoples' opinions; I always have to be happy with the work before I am able to show it to anyone.'

5.8

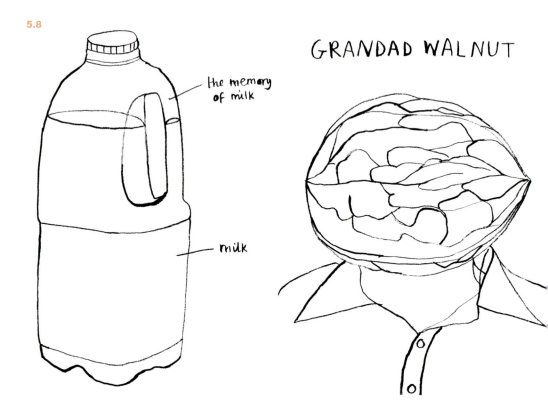

the memory
of milk

milk

GRANDAD WALNUT

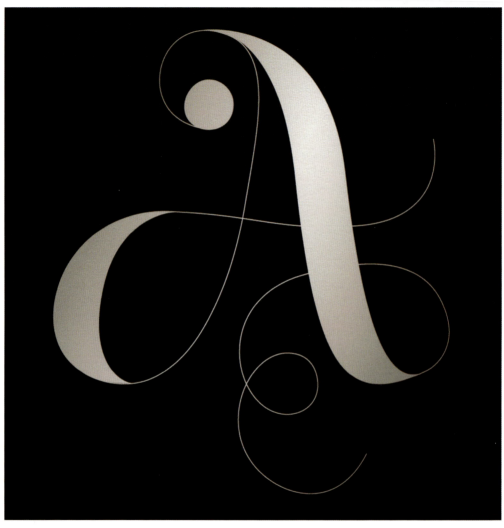

5.10

**5.10—5.13**
**One Custom Letter A Day**
*Simon Ålander*

In order to push his creative limits, Simon Ålander produced one custom letter a day to explore and experiment with letter forms. This project was inspired by LetterCult's 'Alphabattle'.

5.11

5.12

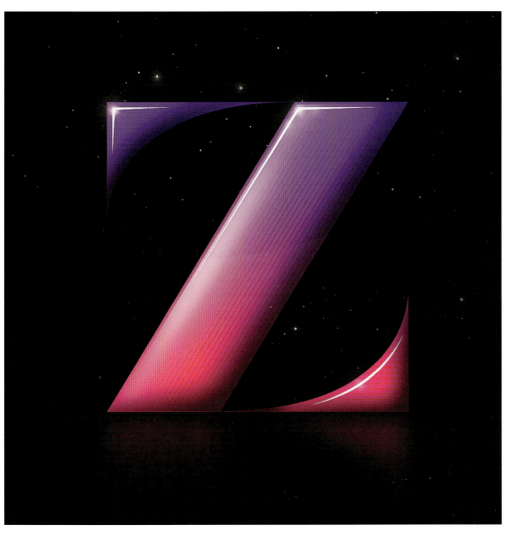

5.13

## Testing

Once you start developing solutions in response to your research findings, you will need to test them rigorously against the goals set in the original brief. Reflection is vital to this process – when testing a piece of design you need to consider why you are getting the results you are getting and how you can use them to progress your designs.

Methods of testing vary, depending on the context of the work, but the basic principles apply to most areas of design. Regardless of the type of product being evaluated, you should always look for a connection with the audience as this is what will sell it.

First, you should test the legibility of a design. Ask the audience what information they have understood from it. You can measure this understanding against your design objectives and then determine how effective your solutions have been – if the audience arrives at the right understanding, the design job has been done well.

When testing material properties associated with a design, it is important that you can simulate proper usage to ensure it will not break, deteriorate or become harmful when used.

Thorough testing will not only help you decide on the usefulness and appropriateness of a concept, but it may also help you generate further ideas. You can test several ideas, and then use the information generated to help you progress your work. Importantly, the work generated through testing will be fit for purpose.

### A good test

To measure the success of any test, there are a few key things that you can look for:

- How quickly do the participants engage with the item being tested?
- Do they appear to be enjoying the process, or do they look stressed or confused?
- Does the conversation within the test group focus on what is being tested?
- Are all of the group members asking questions and actively engaging with the test?

**Audience trials**

An audience trial involves giving consumers a prototype of a product and asking them to report back about its ease of use and potential. This differs from other types of test as it can take place over an extended period and involve the same person looking at several versions of the product, as it is developed.

The audience's engagement will be monitored as well as the item's performance. Designers using audience trials will look specifically for the way a person interacts with their product, and will test this across a number of scenarios and conditions. Even if a product is likely to be used around the house, it will need to be tested against the elements as it is likely to be transported and exposed to harsher conditions at some point.

Many tests can be simulated in a testing laboratory, but human interaction with a product will pick up lots more potential problems. For instance, machines can be used to simulate the gradual wear of shoes, but cannot easily replicate the individual steps of the human foot as it falls on different terrains. A lab test will look for issues of suitability through key use, but an audience trial will push the product to its limits and probably see it being used in ways it's not entirely meant to be.

Sometimes the only thing you can do with a poorly-designed experiment is to try to find out what it died of.

R. A. Fisher

## Usability and user experience testing

When designing a website, it is essential that your audience understand how it works as soon as they log on. Usability and user experience testing is a form of audience trial used exclusively within website design. This tests the audience's ability to understand and access the information in the site.

Websites have certain conventions that are understood by the audience and it is vital to understand these, as your audience will not want to work hard to find their way around. If the navigation and content is not where they expect, they are likely to go to another website to find the products or information they need.

Within web design there are many variables that influence use and access – these are constantly evolving and presenting new challenges. As many people now access the web on mobile phones, the way navigation works has had to evolve alongside this new technology.

A usability test involves an audience member accessing and navigating a prototype of a website, in order to highlight errors or areas that need improvement. The test will be monitored and usually filmed; the person's hand and eye movements can be tracked to see if they are using the site in the way it is intended.

These tests take place in a controlled situation and look initially for performance – the first tests will consider ease of use and accessibility for different audience members. The results of the first test will be used as a baseline, which all subsequent tests will be compared to for improvement purposes.

The design team will also consider whether the tests have evoked the intended emotional response from the users. However useful an object is, there has to be a connection with the audience or they may lose interest and switch to a different product or provider.

**Five is the magic number**
In the early 1990s, usability consultant Jakob Nielsen claimed that five users is enough for usability testing, as little is gained from watching any more than five people suffer through the same flawed design.

Elaborate usability tests are a waste of resources. The best results come from testing no more than five users and running as many small tests as you can afford.

Jakob Nielsen

5.14

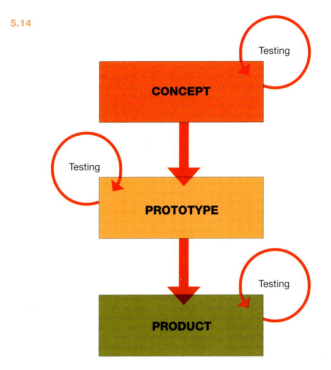

Specific issues usability testing seeks to address include:

- Performance – How much time and how many steps are required for the user to complete basic tasks?

- Accuracy – How many mistakes did they make? Were these mistakes recoverable with the right information or were they fatal?

- Recall – What memory does the user have after periods of non-use?

- Emotional response – How does the person feel emotionally about the tasks completed? Are they confident or stressed? Would they recommend this system to a friend?

**5.14**
As shown in this simplified diagram, testing should occur at every stage of a project. Don't wait until the end of the project – test the concept, test the prototype, test the product.

## Development

When working on any project, you will constantly seek the best results, but research findings cannot simply be meshed together in the hope they will produce a satisfactory solution. Results have to be developed and refined to ensure they work well as a whole.

An idea can be developed in any number of ways, and these will often be particular to and dependent upon the research that you have undertaken. There is often not a right or wrong solution to a brief, but ideas that are developed and informed by strong research are the most likely to succeed.

Further rounds of research and testing can determine what to develop and what the possibilities for advancement are. Once you think you've found a solution, test it and reflect on the results to see which elements need to be developed further. For example, as you are progressing through various stages of your project, many of the research techniques discussed in this book, such as audience tests, focus groups, and material tests, will ensure you are on track. If this development process is considered closely, it will allow you to prove your concepts and highlight areas that might benefit from further investigation. By carefully and deliberately developing your concepts from initial thoughts through to implementation, you will find a successful solution.

5.15

**5.15—5.17**
**Simon Ålander**

Simon mixes both analogue and digital techniques to develop his ideas and designs. The main inspirations for his typography and lettering creations are music, street wear and graffiti.

The hand-drawn Horse Bay Blues poster was inspired by Nikola Sarcevic's song of the same name.

5.16

5.17

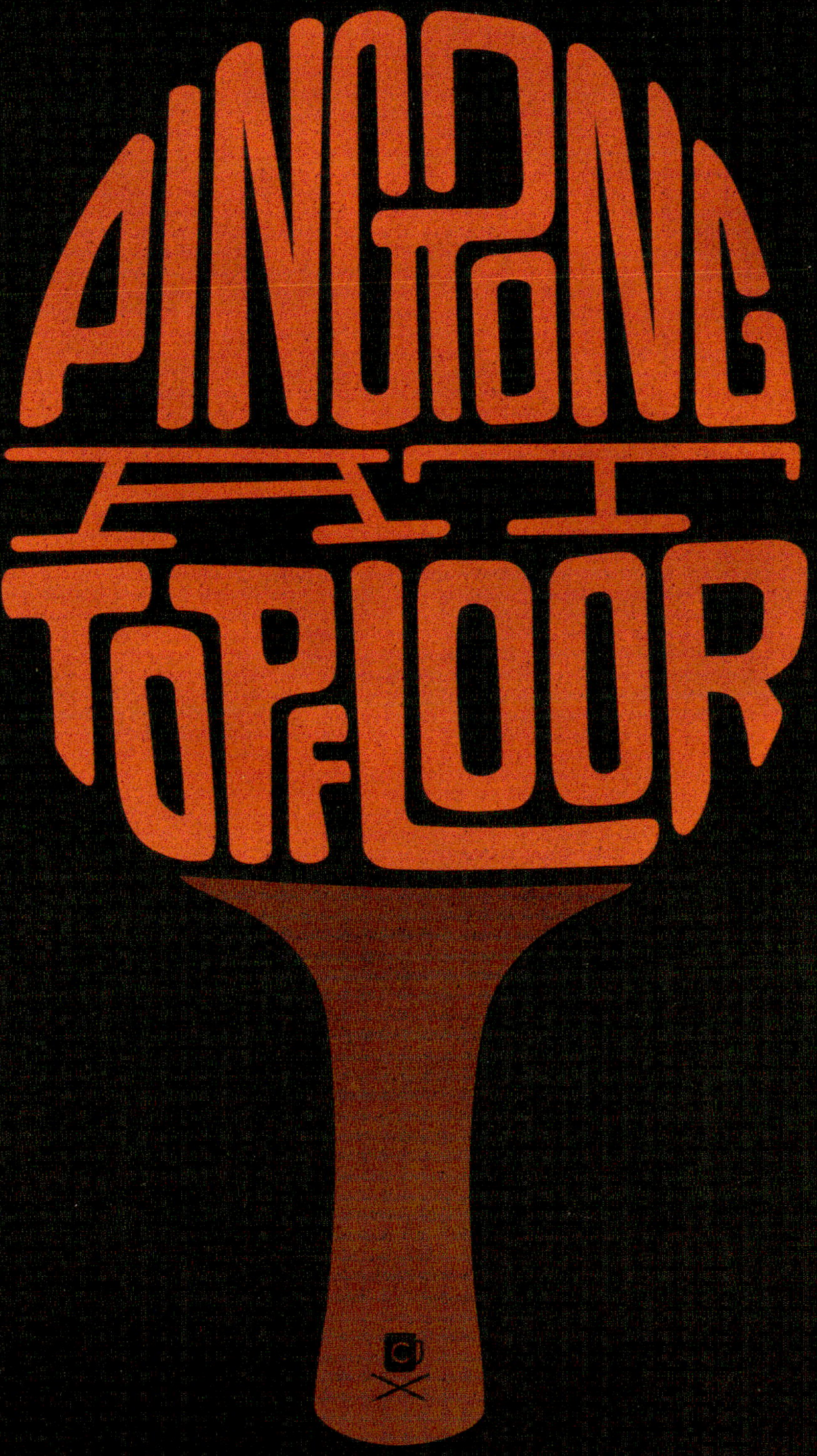

 BILLY BLUE
COLLEGE OF DESIGN®

**ADVENTURE INTO DESIGN**
THINKING | MAKING | CONNECTING

**MELBOURNE, SYDNEY, BRISBANE**
Join us at www.billyblue.edu.au or call 1300 851 245 to find out more

5.19

5.20

**5.18—5.20**
**Billy Blue College of Design, Melbourne**
*Motherbird*

Shown are elements developed to construct an identity for the Billy Blue College of Design in Melbourne, Australia. The eclectic elements create a unique and engaging graphic device as Motherbird explain, 'Working from the starting point of a journey, a narrative was storyboarded with a single frame representing each of Billy Blue's principles: thinking, making and connecting. Paper models were constructed, photographed and retouched, becoming the 'hero' images of the campaign. The result was a series of images that blur the line between tangible and intangible, tactile and digital. Each model was in itself a journey and a labour of love.'

**151**

Underware is a design studio founded in 1999 by Akiem Helmling, Bas Jacobs and Sami Kortemäki who are based in Den Haag, Helsinki and Amsterdam, respectively. Their work has pushed the boundaries of type design, through the development of a series of fonts and publications.

**What does research mean to you?**

Take nothing for granted.

**Where do you start with a brief?**

Most projects we do are self initiated. In this sense, we are very good at keeping ourselves busy by asking difficult questions.

**What methods of research do you find to be most effective?**

To not use a method. We can get very enthusiastic; sometimes overenthusiastic. When this happens we tend to lose sight of the big picture. This prevents us from precisely planning what we are doing. We like to think big, without knowing where that will take us.

Here's one of our goals: to give kudos to our mothers while they're still alive. For that reason they were our three cover girls in the *Is Not Take-away # 1* publication.

**Where do you find inspiration?**

We might get our inspiration from yoga, Karelian pies, riding bikes and waves, watching clouds, Spätzle – culture in its broadest sense – any kind of subculture, jumping in a hole in the ice, German sausages, and a relaxed sauna. We also appreciate our daily chocolate, especially Nutella. All this keeps us going. Yesterday I went to the Botanical Garden and saw two very beautiful plants, with unbelievable shapes. Unheard of. Really amazing.

Regarding type design, all this matters – call it inspiration. But of course, within such a conventional area as text typefaces, you also need to have knowledge about the history of type design and typography. I won't deny that this knowledge can also be inspiring.

5.21

**5.21**
**Type sketches**

**5.22**
**'Is Not take-away # 1' publication**
The prolific output of Underware has had a marked impact on the development of contemporary type design. The production of a series of journals, shown here, helps to showcase and contextualize the typefaces they create.

As we have seen, if your research findings are unordered, it will be unclear what could be of most use, or where patterns and trends occur. Once your research is in order, it is much easier to begin the process of synthesis, continuing lines of enquiry that will be the most productive, and rejecting others.

**Brief**

For this task, you are asked to record and classify a range of information. Using a digital camera, record as many signs as you can on a busy high street.

Once you have a sizeable amount of data to work with you can transfer the images to a page layout programme.

You should then start to look for trends that you can use to categorize them. These may include:

- Typographic style
- Colour
- Use of the sign
- Purpose of the sign
- Intended viewer
- Material
- Position

You may find several different ways to classify a sign that means that you can cross-reference images across selections.

**Project objectives**

- Developing primary research skills.
- Identifying systems that can be used to judge and classify research results.

**Recommended reading related to this project**

Barthes, R (2009). *Mythologies.* Vintage Classics

Chandler, D (2007). *Semiotics: The Basics*. Routledge

Crow, D (2006). *Left to Right: The Cultural Shift from Words to Pictures*. AVA Publishing

Crow, D (2010). *Visible Signs: An Introduction to Semiotics in the Visual Arts.* AVA Publishing

McAlhone, B and Stuart, D (1998). *A Smile in the Mind: Witty Thinking in Graphic Design*. Phaidon Press

Rose, G (2006). *Visual Methodologies: An Introduction to the Interpretation of Visual Materials.* Sage Publications

## Chapter 6 – Presenting your findings

**To conclude, we look at how you can visualize your research findings in ways that clearly communicate the narrative of your research and design process.**

Through this chapter we consider exciting and innovative ways of presenting your findings that will engage the viewer and convince the client that your idea is the right one, from statistical data to models and maquettes. We then look at ways ideas can be successfully developed into viable and worthy outcomes.

**Explaining your research findings can be a complex task, but if this is done effectively it can persuade your client that your solutions are the right ones. You can think of the presentation of your research as an argument – you need to convince the audience that your hypothesis is correct and leave them believing it is the only clear recourse.**

Clarity is the key to effectively presenting research; the findings should be clear, easy to understand and each part should lead from the brief towards your proposed solution. There are many ways you can display your research but the methods you choose should always be appropriate to the audience and not baffle them. To achieve this, you can look at ways of synthesizing large amounts of data using narrative and visualization techniques.

**Client presentations**

It is vital that your client understands the work you have done and the reasons for the choices you have made, as there is always an element of risk for them. It is good practice to keep them well informed, and simple presentations can help you do this. Presentations can take many forms and it is important to understand what should be shown to the client at which point. Initial presentations will often be dialogues, demonstrating the possibilities you can offer, your working methods, specialisms and approach. As the brief progresses, presentations will focus more on refinement until the final designs are shown to the client.

When presenting your results to a client it is important that you are honest, but also keep things simple. An overview that shows the steps you have gone through should suffice and demonstrate that you have considered the feedback you have received, and that it has informed your progress.

**A rough guide to presenting work**

1. Present more than one idea. It is important that the client can see there are different design options.

2. Present all of your ideas with equal vigour and enthusiasm – you don't want it to appear that you are presenting anything you don't believe in.

3. Listen – during the presentation you should be able to learn from others and from their reactions.

4. Ask for feedback and try to get a dialogue going – rather than preaching about the virtues of a design.

5. Keep your presentation simple and concise.

6.1

**6.1**
**One**
*Creasence*

This brand identity presentation, for high-end car distributor One, demonstrates the process designers go through. Shown here (6.1) is early sketch work, that was developed into a series of design options, or 'routes', shown over the following pages.

6.2

6.3

**6.4**

**6.2—6.5**
**One**
*Creasence*

When presenting brand identities, showing them in context can be highly persuasive. Here, three 'routes' were presented in the form of indicative adverts, using aspirational imagery.

Ultimately, a brand is built from several components – the identity is one of these, but imagery, visual language and placement of elements all contribute to its overall success.

Route one, is shown here (6.2).

Route two (6.3) makes use of a strong graphic design.

Route three (6.4 and 6.5) became the final brand identity.

**6.5**

**ONE GmbH**
Variant 1. Logo using example.

## Visualizing data

To ensure that your audience or client understands the research data you have collated, you should consider how best to present it. This does not have to take the form of bar charts and graphs; visualizing data can be a highly creative part of the design process.

There are many ways to present statistics and numbers in visually stimulating ways; from pictorial and photographic illustrations to charts that involve associated facts.

German artist Gerd Arntz (1900–1988) designed a system of 'isotypes' that have been used to display complicated information and statistics. Arntz developed around 4,000 of these icons (see <www.gerdarntz.org>), representing almost every aspect of life, including industry, pastimes and commerce. With these designs, a simplified image of the subject is used to represent a great number. For example, an icon of a man may represent one thousand, making the information more accessible to the viewer than if numbers alone were used.

6.6

6.6
**Homepage Gerd Arntz webarchive**
*<www.gerdarntz.org>*

6.7
**Isotype symbol, Gerd Arntz, 1930s**
*Archive Gemeentemuseum*
*The Hague, The Netherlands*
*www.gerdarntz.org*

6.8
**Isotype linocut and print, Gerd Arntz, 1930s**
*Archive Gemeentemuseum*
*The Hague, The Netherlands*
*Photo: Max Bruinsma*

6.7

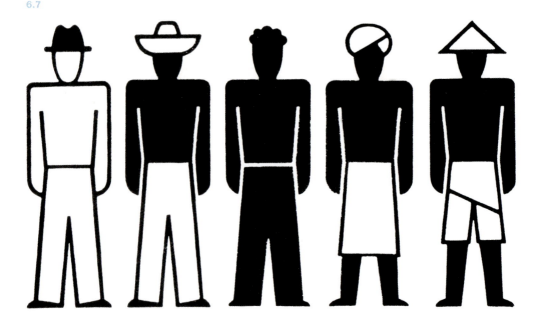

6.8

**6.9—6.10**
**Nostalgic Style**
*Heather Webster* **(a student at the University of Brighton, UK)**

Shown are stills from a short animation that was produced to accompany a series of interviews exploring notions of fashion and nostalgia. The research for this was undertaken with a firsthand approach, directly talking to relatives, friends and the general public. Heather explains 'I find generating conversations with people I don't know very interesting, and this informs how I work. With this project the interviews determined what the artwork would look like and it was fun to respond visually to what was being said through a moving collage.' This aural history is then presented as a series of moving image collages. 'An illustrator has to have a good understanding of type and to know in what context a designer would place their work. The designer also needs to be sympathetic towards the image maker, taking care to complement an image with the layout and treatment of it.'

6.9

6.10

## Statistics

Simple statistics can be a powerful way of presenting convincing conclusions from your research. If you can state that the majority of audience members questioned agreed that your idea is the best way forward, this would be likely to convince your client that you are heading in the right direction. But beware, herein lies a problem!

Although a majority answer would suggest it is the correct one – often called the wisdom of crowds – there are market sectors where this doesn't translate. For example, in food packaging design, market testing generally finds people prefer what they are familiar with, as opposed to being tempted by the design. Equally with magazine advertising, people need to see an advert several times and become familiar with it, before they will act upon it.

Author Daniel Tammet elaborated on this theory in his book *Embracing the Wide Sky*, using the 'Who Wants to be a Millionaire?' scenario. In this instance, there are those who don't know the answer, those who do know the answer, and those who know an answer that is incorrect. This means that the crowd, even if the number that knows the answer is small, will have an advantage in getting the right answer.

When presenting statistics to your client, it is important to be clear how big, and indeed how diverse, a pool they were taken from. If all interviewees are of a similar demographic, then the statistics will be inherently skewed. Clear presentation of statistics will take judgements away from being seen as personal and will allow you to prove your decisions are based on fact. This type of quantitative research attempts to separate personal preference from the needs and desires of the market you are aiming at.

**The Wisdom of Crowds**
This 2004 book by James Surowiecki proposed that a crowd is better at making a decision than a single person. This has been shown in experiments where crowds of people are asked to guess the weight of an object, or the number of jelly-beans in a jar. Although single answers can be wildly wrong, the average of a number of answers is always more accurate.

**6.11—6.13**
**Visualizing statistics**
*Ben Willers* (a student at the University of Lincoln, UK)

Ben Willers's MA design project, shown over the following pages, demonstrates how visually arresting and engaging statistical information can be. Be it TV watching activity, spending patterns or time spent in a supermarket, almost anything can be researched, mapped, and visualized.

6.11
Life

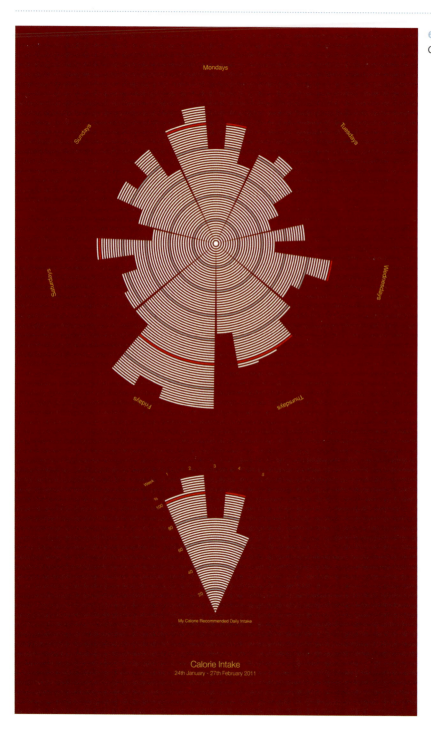

6.12
Calorie intake

6.13
Television
viewing

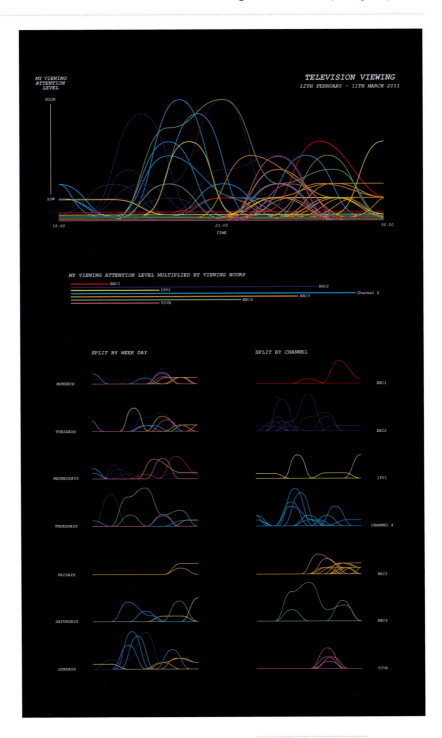

## Narrative

When presenting complex research, is it useful to think of it as a narrative. There is a natural flow to a project – one element should lead to the next and this will draw you to your conclusion. If you can present this to your client, it will help convince them you are correct in your reasoning.

Think about presenting research as a form of storytelling – start at the beginning and guide the reader through. An audience does not always need mountains of detail to convince them; a well-paced narrative with a few key facts and conclusions, presented visually, can be very persuasive.

You can think of the narrative in many different ways. The first thing that comes to most people's mind is a motion-based presentation or a film, but you do not need to use anything this complicated. A paper-based presentation that reiterates the aims of the brief and explains your path and decision making can be just as persuasive.

# A story should have a beginning, a middle and an end… but not necessarily in that order.

Jean-Luc Godard

Presentations can be thought of as visual journeys, delivering surprise and entertainment, while still conveying complex information. It is also worth considering a non-linear narrative, where information isn't necessarily presented in the most obvious order. Often a design presentation will begin with an introduction, then skip to the conclusion, and then go over the main details. This way the value of the conclusion – the most important part – isn't lost.

**Non-linear narrative**
This refers to presenting events out of sequence, or in a disjointed manner. It is said to reflect the way humans remember events, and is a common narrative technique in both literature and film.

**6.14—6.16**
**Project RAR Seen by…**
*Design: Atelier Nunes e Pã*
*Artist: Francisco Vidal*

This annual report for RAR Group is part of an ongoing series that each year commissions an emerging artist from Portugal. The information is clear and delicately set out, but the report goes beyond this, using portraits to add pace, movement and colour.

This is an example of how graphic design often has to do more than one thing. In this case, the primary goal is the clear conveyance of statistical information. Its second purpose is to convey the values, aspirations and direction of the company.

The combination of text and image creates a narrative that the reader can easily navigate.

6.14

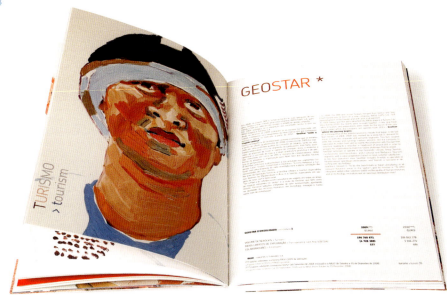

6.15

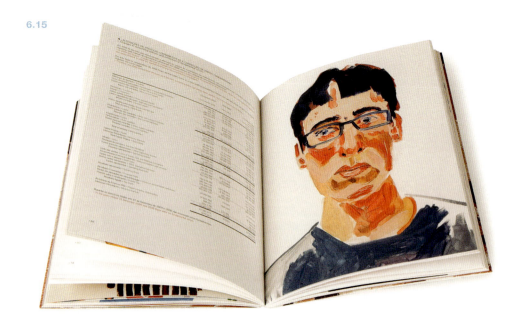

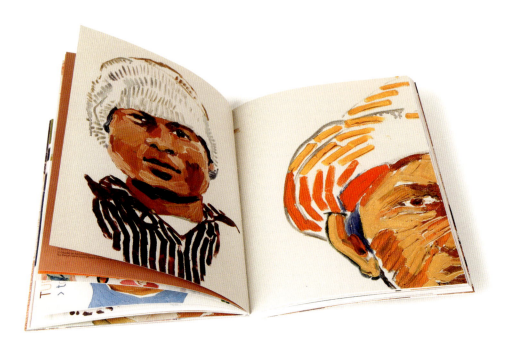

6.16

## Models and maquettes

Maquettes and models are one of the best ways to test the possibilities and durability of material and construction choices, but they are also a great way to demonstrate your idea to a client. A scale model of your idea or final design will say a lot more than a presentation or discussion about an abstract idea.

Traditionally, maquettes and models are associated with three-dimensional projects, but they also work well when presenting a print project such as a book or poster. A model will demonstrate weight, scale and feel – these things can often be hard to simulate in other ways.

By making something that reflects the proportions and finish of your intended final piece, you can test the effectiveness of your ideas by putting it in the environment where it will be seen. This can be a useful tool when asking for feedback from your audience, as they will have something solid to comment on and discuss.

**6.17—6.18**
**Packed**
*Andrew Zo*

Andrew Zo designed an elegant yet practical maquette to house an engagement ring, in a project aptly named 'Packed'. Using various paper materials, Zo used his expertise to craft the ultimate presentation box. What makes it so practical is the fact that it is the size of a credit card and will fit discreetly inside a wallet.

6.17

6.18

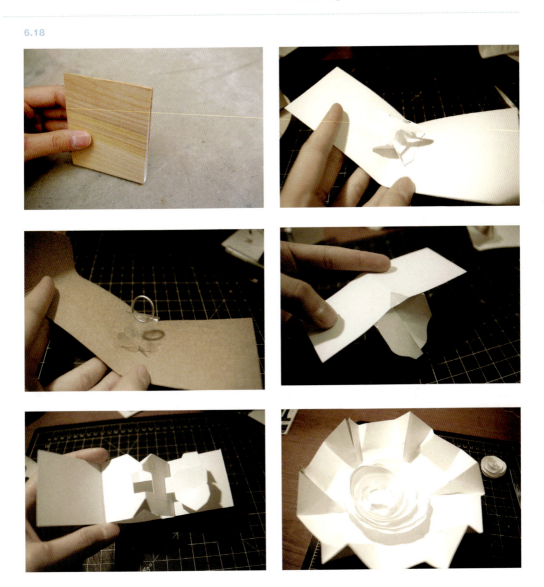

In this particular case study for an engagement ring,
I wanted to provide a jewel case that could be hidden
in a wallet, but when presented, has a surprise element
that mimics a flower blossoming.

Andrew Zo

**It is difficult to know when you have reached the perfect outcome – only your audience and client can tell you this with certainty. If the research you have carried out during your project has been successful, the right people should respond to the product, service, or idea that you are proposing.**

Targeted questioning during the final stages of your project will ensure client satisfaction and give you a chance to respond to any problems before the job has gone too far. This can be viewed as the final stage of research for your project, and getting it right is likely to lead to you gaining further work from the client.

## Questioning the client

While you do not want to grill your client, you need to ensure that you have met their objectives. Take time to gauge their satisfaction. You don't want them to accept work they think is just okay – to get the best from a client/designer relationship, you need to exceed their expectations.

Prepare some points that you would like feedback on, but be careful what you ask – you don't want doubt to enter the client's mind because your questions make you appear unsure about your proposal. Your questions should be phrased to show off the research you have conducted and how you have responded to it – 'We found this out, so we did this; do you think it is effective?'. Evidence-based questions encourage positive responses, leaving little room to be negative or to interject personal preferences.

If the client does not think your proposals work, you will need to ask why and get as much detail as possible. It is important not to take this personally, as they are talking about the work, not you. If you have worked closely with them, it is unlikely that you have missed the mark completely, so don't abandon the proposal entirely. A client may express displeasure for the most minor of reasons, and often these can be remedied with little fuss – the difference between a favourable and unfavourable outcome might be as simple as one colour or typeface choice.

### Questions to ask

When presenting a final design, it is likely to be what the client is looking for – unsuccessful designs rarely make it this far. However, it is well worth evaluating the level of success, as a happy customer is likely to give you more work in the future.

First, always verify that you have met or gone beyond the client's initial aims.

Check for satisfaction – a successful outcome, and one that is liked, can be two different things.

Think ahead – when presenting work, discuss how you think your design work could further develop and enhance the brand, product or service.

After a successful presentation, always ask about further work.

## 6.19—6.20
## Royal Mail Musicals
### *Webb & Webb*

This project to design a set of stamps celebrating the history of British musicals involved a wide range of research methods, including sourcing original posters, utilizing the V&A Theatre Archive and spending time in London's West End.

The resulting stamps are deceptively simple, as James Webb explains: 'Although a stamp design may appear to be a simple photograph or illustration, the work behind the design is extensive and the artwork intricate. There is a rule that living people should not be easily recognizable, so many stamps are built from several layers (see 6.19) to enable subtle masking of visible features without destroying the beauty of the stamp.'

6.19

6.20

## Responding to feedback

Responding to feedback from a client can be either the easiest or hardest part of a project, depending on how detailed their comments are and how well you questioned and understood them.

You may have to look at developing a few 'final' options. Some graphic designers prefer to do this and use the opportunity to gather final feedback. However, presenting too much work may confuse the client, or make you look uncertain. Presenting just one final piece that you are absolutely sure of will demonstrate confidence, but the downside of this is that it may limit your options for success and the client has less to give feedback on. If you have presented more then one solution you will need to listen to the client to determine exactly which parts and elements of each they would like to take forwards.

**6.21—6.22**
**The Manual Co.**
*Peter Gregson Studio*

This packaging by Peter Gregson Studio features a series of illustrations by Vladimir Mirkovic, with design and type treatment by Jovan Trkulja and Filip Bojovic. The hand-drawn, bespoke approach was adopted in response to the nature of the business – a producer of hand-made, high quality leather goods. 'Since the company produces everything manually, the idea was to create packaging in the same spirit,' explains Jovan. Having an understanding of a product's values can help to inform the aesthetics and visual language of a design or brand.

6.21

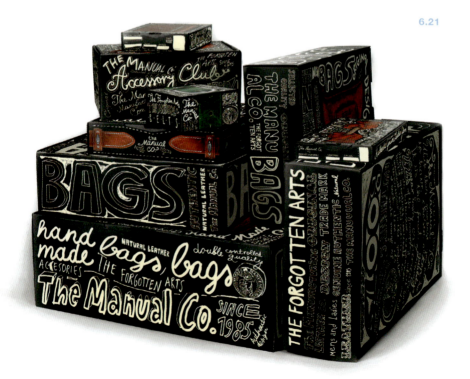

At this point, viability options will be at the forefront of any decisions made. You will need to be realistic – look at the budget again and ensure that you are giving the client what they want for the right price. It is worth formulating a checklist for what needs to be done before the project becomes a fully realized outcome. There are some things you can do such as checking copy, colour values and layouts, but you should also get the client to sign off on these. In a large-scale project with many different parts, there is a greater chance that you will overlook one detail, so it is important to make sure the client checks for any slight discrepancies – otherwise the sole responsibility remains with you.

6.22

## Outcomes

Once the outcome has been agreed there is still the process of dissemination to take into account. Some clients will want to handle this themselves, but it is useful to be part of this process and ensure that your solutions are produced to the highest standards and greeted with the reactions intended.

You will have identified several sources for materials and manufacture during the course of your research as various possibilities were tested, but now further research must begin to provide the client with the best possible outcome for the most competitive price. Depending on the type of project, you will have to consider different providers who can assist with areas such as providing materials, manufacturing, printing and web-hosting.

Once a project is concluded, it is good practice to reflect on the work you have achieved and consider what new skills you have learned and what areas of practice can be developed in time for your next brief.

6.23

**6.23—6.25**
*George Sharp* **(a student at the University of Brighton, UK)**

These beautifully printed posters and cards are the outcome of a process of visual research. There is a clear reference to constructivist themes, while retaining a playful sense of experimentation and visual appeal. 'I was taught to approach a brief as openly as possible; research for a project isn't only when you get the brief, you are always looking for inspiration and ideas. Research for me is establishing the right tone. Most of my influences are found in post-war European designs, especially the constructivist and futurist movements.'

The posters are printed and then cut down to produce other items such as business cards.

6.24

George Sharp
graphic design

07563 349011
www.georgesharp.co.uk
george-sharp@hotmail.com

6.25

**Studio interview:**

**Tanner Christensen**

Tanner Christensen, from Salt Lake City, Utah, is founder of creative ebook publisher Aspindle, and director of online strategy at CLEARLINK.

**What does research mean to you?**

For me, research is walking around the lake that surrounds my office, it's thumbing through an old book, or talking with strangers. It is knowing the important parts of your project, and believing that the best solution can be something entirely unrelated.

Research is branching out, going where you haven't gone before, trying something new, and being someone who isn't afraid to fail. To quote Andre Gide, a favourite French author of mine, 'Man cannot discover new oceans unless he has the courage to lose sight of the shore.'

**Where do you start with a brief?**

There are two key elements of a successful creative brief that must be addressed and completely understood in order to move forward – who is the ideal audience and what do they want? If I can't answer these two questions concisely with help from the client, we can't start. So I always start with these questions, and from there I explore possibilities that might link back to those answers. If you and the client really understand who it is that makes up your audience and what their ultimate goal is, you can do almost anything.

**What methods of research do you find to be most effective?**

Toyota Motor Corporation has an interesting method for solving problems, and I believe the same technique works wonders for research. The method is called 'Five whys' and has you ask 'Why?' at least five times about your project, in succession. In a way, it's a strategy for researching your ideas more than seeking out inspiration – though inspiration certainly comes as a result of understanding the world around us.

Additionally, I personally love exploring ideas and concepts outside of the realm of what it is I am working on specifically. If the project calls for a specific print design, for example, I'll often look to classic film or vintage arcade styles for inspiration. Research is, at it's core, limited only to what you're pursuing.

**6.26**
**Finding order and patterns**

Tanner's creative and personal work manages to find beauty and order in equal measure. A prolific designer and writer, Tanner also publishes a series of books under the banner of Aspindle (www. aspindle.com). Titles such as *Think Unstuck* and *How to Use Ideas* offer a fresh approach to problem solving.

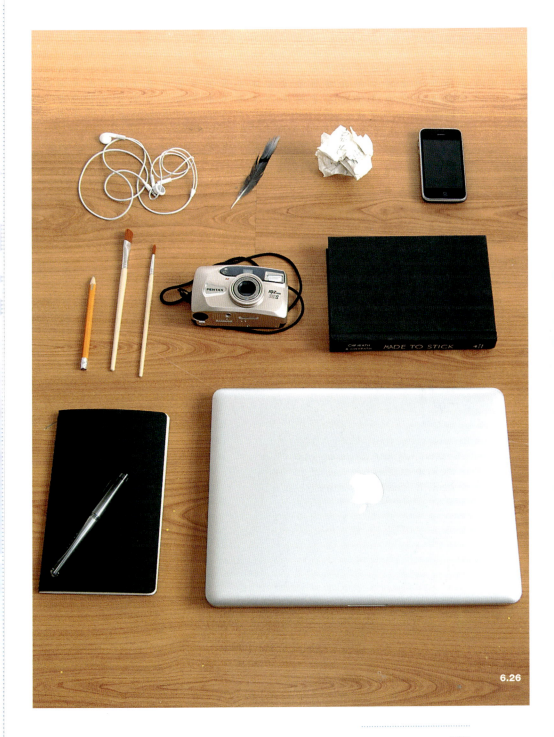

6.26

## Conclusion

**This book aims to provide you with an overview of the varied research methods associated with graphic design. These can be applied whether you are a student, freelancer, or work in a studio.**

We hope this book will help you develop meaningful lines of enquiry in order for you to become the type of designer that approaches each project with an open mind and an inquisitive nature. By employing the approaches detailed in this book you will be able to clearly identify your audience and have a better understanding of the different ways in which you can question and work with them. Asking the right questions of the right people will help you get the best from your projects.

Being a more informed designer will allow you to test your ideas more readily with a clear objective and specific audience in mind. In addition to this, we have discussed terminology that will help give your thinking, ideas and practice greater context. This understanding will help you work towards an active and thorough investigation, getting results that will lead to meaningful and targeted graphic outcomes.

Above all else, it is important to remember that research is not just a process of learning facts; how you interpret the results and use them within your work will be how you find your voice as a designer. Research is a key part of the design process, and will lead to exciting results when done well. The exercises and information contained within this book will help you make the right choices when you approach future projects, and move your work forward in an informed and purposeful manner.

6.26

**Dry statistical information can appear boring and difficult to understand, which makes it a tricky thing to present to a client. This activity encourages you to consider ways of presenting such information so that it is visually engaging for the viewer.**

**Brief**

For this exercise you are asked to research current house prices for your area, and compare them with historical data (this information can easily be found online).

Once you have gathered some statistics, design an innovative and informative presentation that conveys the information in an exciting and engaging way.

When planning this you will need to consider:

- Presenting your findings – which facts are necessary, and what do they indicate that will be of interest?

- Visualizing data – a presentation full of numbers will not engage the viewer; neither will pie charts and graphs. Looking back through the examples in this chapter, what could you bring to the presentation that will represent this information clearly and engage the audience?

- Can you employ a narrative to help make the information more accessible?

- Will the presentation be projected, printed, motion-based, interactive, or will you use props and models to illustrate points?

**Project objectives**

- Understanding the ways research data can be presented to a client.

- Exploring how statistics can be represented with information graphics.

**Recommended reading related to this project**

Ambrose, G and Harris, P (2008). *The Fundamentals of Graphic Design.* AVA Publishing

Draught Associates (2008). *Visual Aid: Stuff You've Forgotten, Things You Never Thought You Knew and Lessons You Didn't Quite Get Around to Learning*. Black Dog Publishing

Draught Associates (2009). *Visual Aid 2: You Can Never Know Enough Stuff*. Black Dog Publishing

Klanten, R, Bourquin, N and Ehmann, S (2010). *Data Flow v. 2: Visualizing Information in Graphic Design*. Die Gestalten Verlag

Kress, G and van Leeuwen, T. (1996). *Reading Images: The Grammar of Visual Design*. Routledge

McCandless, D (2010). *Information is Beautiful.* Collins

Tufte, E (1990). *Envisioning Information.* Graphics Press USA

## Conclusion

**This book aims to provide you with an overview of the varied research methods associated with graphic design. These can be applied whether you are a student, freelancer, or work in a studio.**

We hope this book will help you develop meaningful lines of enquiry in order for you to become the type of designer that approaches each project with an open mind and an inquisitive nature. By employing the approaches detailed in this book you will be able to clearly identify your audience and have a better understanding of the different ways in which you can question and work with them. Asking the right questions of the right people will help you get the best from your projects.

Being a more informed designer will allow you to test your ideas more readily with a clear objective and specific audience in mind. In addition to this, we have discussed terminology that will help give your thinking, ideas and practice greater context. This understanding will help you work towards an active and thorough investigation, getting results that will lead to meaningful and targeted graphic outcomes.

Above all else, it is important to remember that research is not just a process of learning facts; how you interpret the results and use them within your work will be how you find your voice as a designer. Research is a key part of the design process, and will lead to exciting results when done well. The exercises and information contained within this book will help you make the right choices when you approach future projects, and move your work forward in an informed and purposeful manner.

## Contributor contacts

Simon Ålander
coffeemademedoit.com

Gavin Ambrose
gavinambrose.co.uk

Gerd Arntz webarchive
gerdarntz.org

The Miha Artnak
artnak.net

Atelier Nunes e Pã
ateliernunesepa.pt
behance.net/ateliernunesepa

Fabien Barral
fabienbarral.com
mr-cup.com
graphicexchange.com

Ally Carter
allycarter.co.uk

Tanner Christensen
tannerchristensen.com

Tom Clohosy Cole
tomclohosycole.co.uk

Creasence
creasence.com

Matthieu Delahaie
behance.net/dmat64

Chase Farthing
hardworkworks.com

Luciano Ferreira
lucianoferreira.com.br

Fuse Collective
fusecollective.com

Emily Hale
emilyhaledesign.com

Casper Holden
casperholden.com

Andrew Hussey
andrewhussey.co.uk

Randi Sjælland Jensen
behance.net/rsj

Neil Leonard
neilrobertleonard.co.uk

Blake Lowther
blakelowther.com

Ingeborg Lund
ingefaer@hotmail.com

Merlin Mason
merlinmason.co.uk

Motherbird
motherbird.com.au

Studio Output
studio-output.com

Paperlux
paperlux.com

Peter Gregson Studio
petergregson.com
petergregson.com/blog

Planning Unit
planningunit.co.uk

Brian Rea
brianrea.com

Hannah Richards
hannah-richards.co.uk

Serse Rodriguez
serserodriguez.com

Cameron Sandage
cameronsandage.com

George Sharp
georgesharp.co.uk

Castro Smith
castrosmith.blogspot.com

Studio AS
studio_as@o2.co.uk

StudioKxx
studiokxx.com

Morey Talmor
moreytalmor.com

Jane Trustram
janetrustram.com

Underware
underware.nl

Alicia Waters
monkeyinkdesign.com
12ozsteak.com

Webb & Webb
webbandwebb.co.uk

Heather Webster
h-bw.com

Paul Wenham-Clarke
wenhamclarke.co.uk

Ben Willers
lifeindata.site50.net

Xavier Young
xavieryoung.co.uk

Andrew Zo
andrewzodesign.blogspot.com

Lynnie Zulu
lynniezulu.blogspot.com

**Ambrose, G and Harris, P** (2008). *The Fundamentals of Graphic Design*. AVA Publishing

**Arden, P** (2003). *It's Not How Good You Are, It's How Good You Want To Be*. Phaidon Press

**Armstrong, H** (2009). *Graphic Design Theory: Readings from the Field*. Princeton Architectural Press

**Baines, P and Haslam, A** (2002). *Type and Typography*. Laurence King Publishing

**Baldwin, J and Roberts, L** (2006). *Visual Communication: From Theory to Practice*. AVA Publishing

**Barnard, M** (2001). *Approaches to Understanding Visual Culture*. Palgrave

**Barnard, M** (2005). *Graphic Design as Communication*. Routledge

**Barry, P** (2008). *The Advertising Concept Book: Think Now, Design Later*. Thames & Hudson

**Barthes, R** (2009). *Mythologies*. Vintage Classics

**Bennett, A** (2006). *Design Studies: Theory and Research in Graphic Design*. Princeton Architectural Press

**Berger, J** (2008). *Ways of Seeing*. Penguin Modern Classics

**Bergström, B** (2008). *Essentials of Visual Communication*. Laurence King Publishing

**Bierut, M, Drenttel, W and Heller, S** (eds) (2007). *Looking Closer: Bk 5: Critcal Writing on Graphic Design*. Allworth Press

**Burnet, R** (2004). *How Images Think*. MIT Press

**Burtenshaw, K et al.** (2011). *The Fundamentals of Creative Advertising*. AVA Publishing

**Chandler, D** (2007). *Semiotics: The Basics*. Routledge

**Clarke, M** (2007). *Verbalising the Visual: Translating Art and Design into Words*. AVA Publishing

**Crow, D** (2006). *Left to Right: The Cultural Shift from Words to Pictures*. AVA Publishing

**Crow, D** (2010). *Visible Signs: An Introduction to Semiotics in the Visual Arts*. AVA Publishing

**Draught Associates** (2008). *Visual Aid: Stuff You've Forgotten, Things You Never Thought You Knew and Lessons You Didn't Quite Get Around to Learning*. Black Dog Publishing

**Draught Associates** (2009). *Visual Aid 2: You Can Never Know Enough Stuff*. Black Dog Publishing

**Elam, K** (2004). *Grid Systems: Principles of Organizing Type*. Princeton Architectural Press

**Elam, K** (2007). *Typographic Systems*. Princeton Architectural Press

**Eskilson, S** (2007). *Graphic Design: A New History*. Laurence King Publishing

**Fletcher, A** (2001). *The Art of Looking Sideways*. Phaidon Press

**Goddard, A** (2002). *The Language of Advertising: Written Texts*. Routledge

**Graves, P** (2010). *Consumerology: The Market Research Myth, The Truth About Consumer Behaviour and The Psychology of Shopping*. Nicholas Brealey Publishing

**Hall, S** (2007). *This Means This, This Means That: A User's Guide to Semiotics*. Laurence King Publishing

**Hall, S** (ed) (1997). *Representation: Cultural Representations and Signifying Practices*. Sage Publications

**Klanten, R, Bourquin, N and Ehmann, S** (2010). *Data Flow v. 2: Visualizing Information in Graphic Design*. Die Gestalten Verlag

**Klein, N** (2010). *No Logo.* Fourth Estate

**Kress, G and van Leeuwen, T** (1996). *Reading Images: The Grammar of Visual Design*. Routledge

**Lupton, E and Cole Phillips, J** (2008). *Graphic Design: The New Basics*. Princeton Architectural Press

**Malamed, C** (2009). *Visual Language for Designers: Principles for Creating Graphics That People Understand*. Rockport Publishers

**McAlhone, B and Stuart, D** (1998). *A Smile in the Mind: Witty Thinking in Graphic Design*. Phaidon Press

**McCandless, D** (2010). *Information is Beautiful*. Collins

**McLuhan, M, and Fiore, Q** (2008). *The Medium is the Massage: An Inventory of Effects*. Penguin Classics

**Millman, D** (2008). *The Essential Principles of Graphic Design*. Rotovision

**Mono Design** (2005). *Branding: From Brief to Finished Solution*. Rotovision

**Noble, I and Bestley, R** (2002). *Experimental Layout.* Rotovision

**Noble, I and Bestley, R** (2007). *Visual Research: An Introduction to Research Methodologies in Graphic Design*. AVA Publishing

**Pipes, A** (2009). *Production for Graphic Designers*. Laurence King Publishing

**Poynor, R** (2003). *No More Rules: Graphic Design and Postmodernism.* Laurence King Publishing

**Raymond, M** (2010). *The Trend Forecaster's Handbook*. Laurence King Publishing

**Roberts, L** (2005). *Drip-dry Shirts: the Evolution of the Graphic Designer*. AVA Publishing

**Roberts, L** (2006). *Good: An Introduction to Ethics in Graphic Design*. AVA Publishing

**Rose, G** (2006). *Visual Methodologies: An Introduction to the Interpretation of Visual Materials.* Sage Publications

**Sharp, B** (2010). *How Brands Grow: What Marketers Don't Know.* Oxford University Press

**Stephenson, K and Hampshire, M** (2007). *Packaging: Design Successful Packaging for Specific Customer Groups*. Rotovision

**Stone, T** (2010). *Managing the Design Process, Volume 1: Concept Development*. Rockport Publishers

**Sudjic, D** (2009). *The Language of Things: Design, Luxury, Fashion, Art: How We Are Seduced By The Objects Around Us*. Penguin

**Tufte, E** (1990). *Envisioning Information*. Graphics Press USA

**Wigan, M** (2006). *Basics Illustration: Thinking Visually*. AVA Publishing

Page numbers in *italics* denote illustration captions.

advertising strategies 110
aesthetics 52
Ålander, Simon 88, *140*, *148*
Ambrose, Gavin *42*, *103*
analytical research 31
archives, images 88
Arntz, Gerd 162, *162*
art movements 50–51, 52
art nouveau 50
Artnak, The Miha *136*
Arts and Crafts Movement 50
Atelier Nunes e Pã *82*, *170*
audience trials 145
audiences 10
    and clients 70
    conducting research 96–98, 100, 102, 104–105
        contexts 38–46, 54
        descriptive research 29
        planning work 76–77
        primary research 22
        qualitative research 28
        testing findings 144–147
avant-garde 50, 51

Ballinger, Gemma *119*
Banksy *117*
Barral, Fabien *72*
Barthes, Roland 62
*Big Issue, The 112*
Billy Blue College of Design *151*
blogs 57, 78, 88, *88*
Bojovic, Filip *178*
briefs 14, 70–72
Buczkowski, Piotr *10*
buying choices 124

Carter, Ally *78*, *86*
case studies 105
categorization 128
Christensen, Tanner *182*
classification 154–155
client presentations 158
clients 14, 70, 96, 158, 176
Cole, Tom Clohosy *6*
*Computer Arts Collection* magazine *48*
conducting research 95–125
        audience research 96–98, 100, 102, 104–105
        field-based research 112, 117–118

market research 106–108, 110
        process-based research 120
connotation 62
construction 120
constructivism 51
consumer reviews 106–107
content analysis 132
contexts 37–67
        design contexts 50–60
        social contexts 38–46
        theories 60–62
controlled experimentation 136
convenience sampling 100
convention (sign) 62
conventions (markets) 66
coolhunting 29, 117
copyright, images 88
Creasance *159*, *161*
credibility, information sources 78
crowdsourcing 118, 166

data, visualizing 162
data resources 22
de Bono, Edward 30
Delahaie, Matthieu *74*
demographic 42
denotation 62
descriptive research 29
design contexts 50–60
design movements 50–51
developing ideas 148
Dixon, Chris *90*
documenting work 82, 88

Earth Music Bristol *64*
Ecko Unltd. *110*
economic climate 38
end-users 76, 77, 92
ethics 46, 97
experimentation 136

Farthing, Chase *98*
fashion cycles 57, *57*
feedback 178–179
Ferreira, Luciano *41*
field-based research 112, 117–118
fieldwork 112
findings *see* presenting findings; using findings
Fleming & Howland *42*
focus groups 104
forms 28
Fuller, Richard Buckminster *57*
Fuse Collective *44*, *110*

futurism 51

global communities 40
green politics 46

Habit *107*
Hale, Emily *26*, *32*, *32*, *134*
Hannah Turner Ceramics *114*
Harvard referencing system 80
Helmling, Akiem *152*
historical context 50–51
Holden, Casper *120*
Howe, Jeff 118
Hussey, Andrew 64, *64*, *114*

icons 62, *62*
identity 42
images 88
Impressionism 50
index 62, *62*
information, sources of 12, 78, 80
Internet 23, 57, 78, 88, 118
interviews 82, 102
isotypes 162, *162*

Jacobs, Bas *152*
Jensen, Randi Sjælland *120*
jobs, obtaining 14, 88
Joupii *12*

Kamen, Dean *57*
Koons, Jeff *51*
Kortemäki, Sami *152*

Lasswell, Harold 132
lateral thinking 30
Laver, James 57, *57*
Leeds Design for Activism Festival poster 38
Leonard, Neil *112*
libraries 12, 23
local contexts 40
Lowther, Blake *47*
Lund, Ingeborg *120*

Magritte, René 63, *63*
Manual Co., The *179*
market leaders 108
market research 106–108, 110
marketing strategies 108
Mason, Merlin *38*
materials 120
McLuhan, Marshall 40
methodology 72
methods, research 18, 22–23
Mirkovic, Vladimir *178*

models 174
modernism 51
Monkey Ink Design 24
Montreal Biosphere 57
Morris, William 51
Motherbird 151
Mountain Man 26

narrative 170
New York magazine 90
New York Times magazine 32
Nielsen, Jakob 146
non-linear narrative 170
non-participant observation 97
non-probability sampling 100
Novum magazine 58

observation 14, 29, 97
One 159, 161
online resources, documenting work 88
open-ended experimentation 136
outcomes 180
overview, projects 14

Paperlux 58
participant observation 97
Peirce, Charles Sanders 62
Peter Gregson Studio 178
physical resources, documenting work 82
Planning Unit 48
planning work 69–93
    audience 76–77
    briefs 70–72
    documenting 82, 88
    information sources 78, 80
pointillism 50
politics 46
postmodernism 51
preparatory research 14
presenting findings 157–185
    client presentations 158
    models 174
    narrative 170
    statistics 166
    visualizing data 162
primary audience research 22
primary research 18, 22
probability sampling 100
process-based research 120
production 10, 120
propositional research 30
pure research 30

qualitative research 26, 28–29

quantitative research 26, 28
questioning clients 176
questionnaires 28, 98, 132

Rams, Dieter 55
RAR Group 170
Rea, Brian 90, 90, 101
recording work 82, 88
referencing information 80
reflection 96, 130, 148, 180
reflexivity 96
research (basics of) 9–35, 186
    and design process 18
    methods 18, 22–23
    need for 10
    as ongoing process 6
    stages of 70
    starting 12–14
    successful 26
    terminology 26, 28–31
responding to findings 134, 136, 144–148
reviews, tertiary research 23
Richards, Hannah 2, 138
Robert Adam Architects 12, 76
Robertson, Raine Manley 134
Rodriguez, Serse 130
Royal Mail Musicals 177
Rubens, Peter Paul 55, 55

sampling 100
Sandage, Cameron 98
Santos, Marco Dos 74
Saussure, Ferdinand de 60
secondary research 18, 22
Segway Personal Transporter 57
semiotics 31, 60, 62–63
Sharp, George 180
signifiers 60
signs 60, 62
sketching 18, 22, 82
skim boards 44
Smith, Castro 18
social contexts 38–46
social media 57, 119
Sonae group 82
stages of research 70
starting research 12–14
statistics 28, 29, 166, 184
Studio AS 15, 16, 17
Studio Output 119
StudioKxx 10
styles 54
successful research 26
Surowiecki, James 166
surveys 28, 100, 132

SWOT analysis 108, 108
symbols 62, 62
synthesis 129

Talmor, Morey 80, 107
Tekël 74
terminology 26, 28–31
tertiary research 18, 23
testing, audiences 77, 144–147
theories 60–62
topography 128
trends 54, 57, 117
trendspotting 29, 117
tribal art 52
Trkulja, Jovan 178
Trustram, Jane 122, 122
Turner, Hannah 114
Twitter 119
typefaces 54
typology 128

UK Fashion Hub 103
Underware 152, 152
UNIQLO 130
usability testing 146–147
user experience testing 146
using findings 127–155
    responding to 134, 136, 144–148
    understanding 128–130, 132–133

Vanbrugh Court 15, 16, 17
vernacular 44
Vidal, Francisco 170
visualizing data 162

Waters, Alicia 24
Webb, James 12, 177
Webb & Webb 12, 76, 177
websites 57, 78
Webster, Heather 164
Wenham-Clarke, Paul 112
Willers, Ben 166

Young, Xavier 42

Zo, Andrew 174
Zulu, Lynnie 52

## Acknowledgements

**Thank you to Sarah, Mary, Phil and Rachel Leonard, Katie and Manuel Cruz, Paul Allen, Henry Brown, Neil Mabbs, Jacqui Sayers, Leafy Cummins, Sarah Turner, Gavin Ambrose, The Arts University College at Bournemouth Visual Communication team (past and present) and all of the students I have worked with who inspired this book.**

The publisher would like to thank Barrie Tullett, Graham Jones and Simon Gomes for their comments on the manuscript.


Image credits:

Cover image by Fuse Collective
p11 The Energy Within Me, © StudioKxx 2011
p23 1.10 and 1.12, © Jirsak/Shutterstock.com
p23 1.11, © lightpoet/Shutterstock.com
p26 Mountain Man, © Emily Hale 2010
p33 Does the Type of Disaster Change What Matters? © Emily Hale 2010
p51 Jeff Koons, Puppy, © Toni Sanchez Poy/Shutterstock.com
p56 Montreal Biosphere, © Massimiliano Pieraccini/Shutterstock.com
p57 Segway Personal Transporter, © Segway Inc.
p62 Horse diagram, © Dover Press
p116 Banksy, Hanging Man, © 1000 Words/Shutterstock.com
p134 Harvey Milk Wine, photographed by Raine Manley Robertson,
© Emily Hale 2010
p160 6.2, © Max Eary/Shutterstock.com
p160 6.3, © ARENA Creative/Shutterstock.com
p161 6.5, © Max Eary/Shutterstock.com
p162 Gerd Arntz isotypes, www.gerdarntz.org, initiative: Ontwerpwerk
(www.ontwerpwerk.nl), texts: Max Bruinsma (www.maxbruinsma.nl).
© Gerd Arntz c/o Pictoright Amsterdam, 2008, www.pictoright.nl

All reasonable attempts have been made to trace, clear and credit the copyright holders of the images reproduced in this book. However, if any credits have been inadvertently omitted, the publisher will endeavour to incorporate amendments in future editions.

## Publisher's note

The subject of ethics is not new, yet its consideration within the applied visual arts is perhaps not as prevalent as it might be. Our aim here is to help a new generation of students, educators and practitioners find a methodology for structuring their thoughts and reflections in this vital area.

AVA Publishing hopes that these **Working with ethics** pages provide a platform for consideration and a flexible method for incorporating ethical concerns in the work of educators, students and professionals. Our approach consists of four parts:

The **introduction** is intended to be an accessible snapshot of the ethical landscape, both in terms of historical development and current dominant themes.

The **framework** positions ethical consideration into four areas and poses questions about the practical implications that might occur. Marking your response to each of these questions on the scale shown will allow your reactions to be further explored by comparison.

The **case study** sets out a real project and then poses some ethical questions for further consideration. This is a focus point for a debate rather than a critical analysis so there are no predetermined right or wrong answers.

A selection of **further reading** for you to consider areas of particular interest in more detail.

**Ethical:** aware-
ness/
reflect-
ion/
debate

**Working with ethics**

## Introduction

Ethics is a complex subject that interlaces the idea of responsibilities to society with a wide range of considerations relevant to the character and happiness of the individual. It concerns virtues of compassion, loyalty and strength, but also of confidence, imagination, humour and optimism. As introduced in ancient Greek philosophy, the fundamental ethical question is: *what should I do?* How we might pursue a 'good' life not only raises moral concerns about the effects of our actions on others, but also personal concerns about our own integrity.

In modern times the most important and controversial questions in ethics have been the moral ones. With growing populations and improvements in mobility and communications, it is not surprising that considerations about how to structure our lives together on the planet should come to the forefront. For visual artists and communicators, it should be no surprise that these considerations will enter into the creative process.

Some ethical considerations are already enshrined in government laws and regulations or in professional codes of conduct. For example, plagiarism and breaches of confidentiality can be punishable offences. Legislation in various nations makes it unlawful to exclude people with disabilities from accessing information or spaces. The trade of ivory as a material has been banned in many countries. In these cases, a clear line has been drawn under what is unacceptable.

But most ethical matters remain open to debate, among experts and lay-people alike, and in the end we have to make our own choices on the basis of our own guiding principles or values. Is it more ethical to work for a charity than for a commercial company? Is it unethical to create something that others find ugly or offensive?

Specific questions such as these may lead to other questions that are more abstract. For example, is it only effects on humans (and what they care about) that are important, or might effects on the natural world require attention too?

Is promoting ethical consequences justified even when it requires ethical sacrifices along the way? Must there be a single unifying theory of ethics (such as the Utilitarian thesis that the right course of action is always the one that leads to the greatest happiness of the greatest number), or might there always be many different ethical values that pull a person in various directions?

As we enter into ethical debate and engage with these dilemmas on a personal and professional level, we may change our views or change our view of others. The real test though is whether, as we reflect on these matters, we change the way we act as well as the way we think. Socrates, the 'father' of philosophy, proposed that people will naturally do 'good' if they know what is right. But this point might only lead us to yet another question: *how do we know what is right?*

## You
### What are your ethical beliefs?

Central to everything you do will be your attitude to people and issues around you. For some people, their ethics are an active part of the decisions they make every day as a consumer, a voter or a working professional. Others may think about ethics very little and yet this does not automatically make them unethical. Personal beliefs, lifestyle, politics, nationality, religion, gender, class or education can all influence your ethical viewpoint.

Using the scale, where would you place yourself? What do you take into account to make your decision? Compare results with your friends or colleagues.

## Your client
### What are your terms?

Working relationships are central to whether ethics can be embedded into a project, and your conduct on a day-to-day basis is a demonstration of your professional ethics. The decision with the biggest impact is whom you choose to work with in the first place. Cigarette companies or arms traders are often-cited examples when talking about where a line might be drawn, but rarely are real situations so extreme. At what point might you turn down a project on ethical grounds and how much does the reality of having to earn a living affect your ability to choose?

Using the scale, where would you place a project? How does this compare to your personal ethical level?

01  02  03  04  05  06  07  08  09  10

01  02  03  04  05  06  07  08  09  10

## Your specifications
### What are the impacts of your materials?

In relatively recent times, we are learning that many natural materials are in short supply. At the same time, we are increasingly aware that some man-made materials can have harmful, long-term effects on people or the planet. How much do you know about the materials that you use? Do you know where they come from, how far they travel and under what conditions they are obtained? When your creation is no longer needed, will it be easy and safe to recycle? Will it disappear without a trace? Are these considerations your responsibility or are they out of your hands?

Using the scale, mark how ethical your material choices are.

## Your creation
### What is the purpose of your work?

Between you, your colleagues and an agreed brief, what will your creation achieve? What purpose will it have in society and will it make a positive contribution? Should your work result in more than commercial success or industry awards? Might your creation help save lives, educate, protect or inspire? Form and function are two established aspects of judging a creation, but there is little consensus on the obligations of visual artists and communicators toward society, or the role they might have in solving social or environmental problems. If you want recognition for being the creator, how responsible are you for what you create and where might that responsibility end?

Using the scale, mark how ethical the purpose of your work is.

01  02  03  04  05  06  07  08  09  10

01  02  03  04  05  06  07  08  09  10

Working with ethics

One aspect of graphic design that raises an ethical dilemma is that of its relationship with the creation of printed materials and the environmental impacts of print production. For example, in the UK, it is estimated that around 5.4 billion items of addressed direct mail are sent out every year and these, along with other promotional inserts, amount to over half a million tonnes of paper annually (almost 5 per cent of the UK consumption of paper and board). Response rates to mail campaigns are known to be between 1–3 per cent, making junk mail arguably one of the least environmentally friendly forms of print communication. As well as the use of paper or board, the design decisions to use scratch-off panels, heavily coated gloss finishes, full-colour ink-intensive graphics or glues for seals or fixings make paper more difficult to recycle once it has been discarded. How much responsibility should a graphic designer have in this situation if a client has already chosen to embark on a direct mail campaign and has a format in mind? Even if designers wish to minimise the environmental impacts of print materials, what might they most usefully do?

In 1951, Leo Burnett (the famous advertising executive known for creating the Jolly Green Giant and the Marlboro Man) was hired to create a campaign for Kellogg's new cereal, Sugar Frosted Flakes (now Frosties in the UK and Frosted Flakes in the US). Tony the Tiger, designed by children's book illustrator Martin Provensen, was one of four characters selected to sell the cereal. Newt the Gnu and Elmo the Elephant never made it to the shelves and after Tony proved more popular than Katy the Kangaroo, she was dropped from packs after the first year.

Whilst the orange-and-black tiger stripes and the red kerchief have remained, Provensen's original design for Tony has changed significantly since he first appeared in 1952. Tony started out with an American football-shaped head, which later became more rounded, and his eye colour changed from green to gold. Today, his head is more angular and he sits on a predominantly blue background. Tony was initially presented as a character that walked on all fours and was no bigger than a cereal box. By the 1970s, Tony's physique had developed into a slim and muscular six-foot-tall standing figure.

Between 1952 and 1995 Kellogg's are said to have spent more than USD$1 billion promoting Frosted Flakes with Tony's image, while generating USD$5.3 billion in gross US sales. But surveys by consumer rights groups such as Which? find that over 75 per cent of people believe that using characters on packaging makes it hard for parents to say no to their children. In these surveys, Kellogg's come under specific scrutiny for Frosties, which are said to contain one third sugar and more salt than the Food Standards Agency recommends. In response, Kellogg's have said: 'We are committed to responsibly marketing our brands and communicating their intrinsic qualities so that our customers can make informed choices.'

Food campaigners claim that the use of cartoon characters is a particularly manipulative part of the problem and governments should stop them being used on less healthy children's foods. But in 2008, spokespeople for the Food and Drink Federation in the UK, said: 'We are baffled as to why Which? wants to take all the fun out of food by banning popular brand characters, many of whom have been adding colour to supermarket shelves for more than 80 years.'

**Is it more ethical to create promotional graphics for 'healthy' rather than 'unhealthy' food products?**

**Is it unethical to design cartoon characters to appeal to children for commercial purposes?**

**Would you have worked on this project, either now or in the 1950s?**

**I studied graphic design in Germany, and my professor emphasised the responsibility that designers and illustrators have towards the people they create things for.**

**Eric Carle (illustrator)**

AIGA
*Design Business and Ethics*
2007, AIGA

Eaton, Marcia Muelder
*Aesthetics and the Good Life*
1989, Associated University Press

Ellison, David
*Ethics and Aesthetics in European Modernist Literature:*
*From the Sublime to the Uncanny*
2001, Cambridge University Press

Fenner, David E W (Ed)
*Ethics and the Arts:*
*An Anthology*
1995, Garland Reference Library of Social Science

Gini, Al and Marcoux, Alexei M
*Case Studies in Business Ethics*
2005, Prentice Hall

McDonough, William and Braungart, Michael
*Cradle to Cradle:*
*Remaking the Way We Make Things*
2002, North Point Press

Papanek, Victor
*Design for the Real World:*
*Making to Measure*
1972, Thames & Hudson

United Nations Global Compact
*The Ten Principles*
www.unglobalcompact.org/AboutTheGC/TheTenPrinciples/index.html